QUE
ASIE
marmoratus
multiflora
biserrata
Ficus erecta
Pteris cretica
Iris japonica
CW00550338

The Vertical Garden

Patrick Blanc

FROM NATURE TO THE CITY

PREFACE BY JEAN NOUVEL

PHOTOGRAPHS BY THE AUTHOR
AND VÉRONIQUE LALOT

TRANSLATION BY GREGORY BRUHN

W. W. NORTON & COMPANY
NEW YORK • LONDON

CONTENTS

1 Natural habitats

2 The impact of plants on architecture

3 The vertical garden

PREFACE

The Green Man

About fifteen years ago, I met an uncommon and fascinating man. His solid reputation as a scientist and researcher preceded him, a living encyclopedia on plants worldwide—growing in severe and difficult conditions, deprived of light in the shadows of tall trees (where, in contrast to the old saying, there is always something growing), or deprived of nutrients among rocks.... Here was a man who was familiar with strolling the Amazon forests and riding the canopy on a raft. This was thanks to Hervé Chandès, the director of the Cartier Foundation. In the framework of an exhibit, "Being Nature," he had had the unique idea of considering this biology professor as an artist.

His intuition was proven correct, since Patrick Blanc–the Green Man–has drawn results from his endless observations. The process that he created allows plants, flowers, mosses, vines, and shrubs to grow without soil, along the face of a wall. They attach their roots to a mesh-covered felt soaked with mineralized water.

The principal idea behind the Cartier Foundation's exhibit was to create a two-faced vertical garden 20 feet by 10 feet (6 by 3 m), over the main entrance both inside and out. Later, Patrick Blanc brought me to Vincennes and introduced me to his point of reference at the Parc Floral, a steep embankment where, for years, plants had grown heartily, despite sharp winter frosts and glaring summer sun.

As soon as I saw the completed project at the Cartier Foundation, I immediately understood that what I had hoped for had become reality. The vertical gardens could develop from this simple technique and allow flowers, grasses, and fig trees to flourish under shady cedars! We quickly decided, along with Hervé Chandès, to keep the outside part of this garden work of art, since the bookstore sadly prevented us from maintaining one side of the wall indoors. The foundation's architecture was based on vegetation reflecting on the building's walls. Adding a real veil of plants to the building highlighted the ambiguity that I had hoped to create.

This technique opened the way to new possibilities for my projects, and I dream of seeing one of these mysterious walls come to fruition on a much grander scale. Their mystery draws upon Patrick Blanc's extensive research as to which plants can flourish. He works on including a multiplicity of species before installing the ecosystem. Certain heartier or better-adapted plants replace others; others invite themselves into the layout. The system is fabulous, and the results mysterious.

Patrick has become increasingly determined in designing his compositions. For example, a rather prestigious house that I created in Seoul is home to veritable outdoor tapestries stretching 50, 65, 100 feet (15, 20, 30 m). For my project at the French Embassy in Berlin, the interior of that compound was to contrast strongly with the mineral Pariser Platz. Walls reaching 328 feet (100 m) long and 115 feet (35 m) high were to be taken over by plants, and the terraces as well. That project was not completed, but others of the same magnitude will surely come.

A new element has been added to the architectural lexicon. A scientist has given rise to the integration of pleasing new sequences into architectural designs that, in today's environment, are in desperate need of them. This new vocabulary must continue to be enriched. This green art must be underscored by architectural concepts, which it must in turn supplement. It is through this reciprocity that Patrick Blanc will nourish our cultural heritage. The depth of his scientific knowledge will guide him.

JEAN NOUVEL

In the Canary Islands, certain Composites have evolved into quasi-arborescent growth habits, reminiscent of the giant *Senecio* in the East African mountains. I first discovered these plants in the field in August 2007. This *Sonchus ortunoi* on the island of La Gomera grows on the steep slopes of the laurel forest understory (these humid forests are relics of the Tertiary Era and have a wealth of trees of the Lauraceae family). This species has a single whorl of large, lobed leaves at the end of a long stem reaching up to 6 feet (2m) long. It is similar to a number of small shrubs in the tropical rainforest understory.

Facing page:
What a pleasure it was to discover in Borneo, during a field trip in summer 2005, *Cryptocoryne longicauda* growing by the thousands in the swampy zones of the understory in the Gunung Mulu National Park! I had read literature on this plant as an adolescent, but I had never seen it grown in aquariums or in botanical gardens. It grows in highly acidic, still waters less than 4 inches (10cm) deep. When it blooms, only the open part of the spathe (it is an Araceae, from the same family as *Arum* or *Anthurium*) emerges above the waterline, allowing insects to reach the water-tight tube and to fertilize the flowers that remain submerged within an open cavity at the base of the spathe.

The Origins of the Vertical Garden

From the age of five, I was quite taken with the large tropical aquarium in our family doctor's waiting room. I was living in completely urban surroundings, in an apartment in the Parisian suburbs. Contemplating this aquarium, which must have been about six feet long (at least in my memory!), transported me into another world. I was fascinated by the abundance of plants and the variety of fish, which were mostly quite small. Most important, I would spend countless minutes standing and listening to the strange compartment attached to the aquarium, which housed an intense rushing of water. An angled glass tube brought water into the reservoir and sent it streaming back into the aquarium through another vastly more complex glass tube lined with air bubbles pulling the water along. By questioning the doctor, I found out that this strange yet dynamic compartment was the filter, purifying the aquarium's water and maintaining its biological balance. I soon asked my mother for permission to set up something similarly magical at home. On a much more modest scale, my first aquarium allowed me to understand the notion of an ecosystem, even though my ears had not yet heard that term. In fact, the little fish that I enjoyed so much were tropical. It was therefore necessary to gently warm the aquarium with an electrical heater. On top of that, the undulating aquatic plants needed light to grow. I was still unaware of photosynthesis, yet it was necessary to light the plants artificially for twelve hours every day so they could grow. Finally, excess food and fish excrement had to be mechanically evacuated by means of that fascinating filter. Of course, at the age of seven or eight (yes, time had passed before my first attempts were successful!), you don't quite feel like a god, but nonetheless, there is a certain pride to be felt in recreating what seems like a slice of the natural world.

My fascination with aquatic life moved beyond the aquarium. Like most children, I loved collecting tadpoles from the swamps in the springtime, watching their metamorphosis in the aquarium, and then releasing the small frogs into their natural habitat. In the end I always maintained a fine balance between orchestrating the elements necessary for recreating the basic conditions of natural habitats within my home and immersing myself in the habitats themselves. This was also how I approached birds. I never liked large birds in small cages. My parents took me to buy coral-beaked waxbills (known as astrilds or *bengalis*) at the bird market in Paris. Every Thursday and Sunday morning, I would let the birds free, allowing them to fly around the apartment before returning them to their cage. And so I would spend hours watching them fly, a bit fearful that they might crash into the windows. Of course, I was really only granting them the illusion of freedom. But what a pleasure for a young child to observe their curiosity, their fear, and their impulses to fly off into another room or toward another improbable perch, high up on the furniture. I understood that all living animals – fish, frogs, and birds – were endowed with free will. Unconsciously, I already knew that my life would revolve around these confrontations (were they communions?) between free living beings and my own life as a human being bound to city life. I never liked the countryside and never liked gardens (except, of course, botanical gardens). I really only enjoyed cities, big cities, and the most undisturbed natural habitats. Fortunately, my entire imagination has been consistent with my life: I have still only ever lived in cities and for thirty-five years I have traveled the world's most primitive forests.

The first memories that led me toward vertical gardens are probably rooted in two places: the waterfalls in the Bois de Boulogne and the 1964

International Flower Show of Paris. Between the ages of eight and twelve I spent every Thursday with my mother in one of two ways. Half the time, we would stroll the Champs-Élysées, with an obligatory stop on the corner of Rue de la Boétie where we would buy rice to throw to the pigeons. We would then continue our route along the gardens, ending up at the Grands Magasins. Other days, my father would drop us off near the large lake in the Bois de Boulogne and we would return to Suresnes on foot. Along the way, the only park that truly interested me was lined with a string of small brooks and waterfalls in the forest understory. I didn't know, of course, that these six- to nine-foot waterfalls had been created by men. I adored the soft flow resonating off the rocks, giving life to mosses and other plants that were developing in the shade of the trees. These were, in fact, my first encounters with vertical gardens. During the 1964 International Flower Show at La Défense in Paris, I was eleven years old. What a shock! I already had a vague knowledge of Orchidaceae, Bromeliaceae, and Araceae, which I cultivated or had seen at florists. Yet here were these tall trees brimming with epiphytes, waterfalls with fake rocks encrusted in moss and *Nepenthes,* and embankments covered in *Tillandsia.* Each of these visions was a revelation for me. I had become more receptive since the previous summer; I had visited the great greenhouse in Lisbon's botanical garden, which was so rich with full-grown *Philodendron* and *Monstera,* and tall tree ferns. It was probably at that time, during my early high school years, that I started collecting a few Araceae with their luxuriant foliage.

But my main interest remained tropical aquariums, and I tried hard to reproduce species reputed to be difficult, such as angelfish. My sole source of knowledge came from reading expert journals. When I was thirteen, I met up with an acquaintance from my city, Philippe Vallette, and we began to exchange daily observations concerning our successes and failures in reproducing African fish of the *Aphyosemion* genus. Since then, he has become the director of the Nausicaa Aquarium in Boulogne-sur-Mer, where we recently met up to design several unconventionally designed vertical gardens. But whereas Philippe has remained within the realm of fish, I have migrated more and more toward the realm of aquatic plants. At the end of the 1960s, "aquarium" plants began to be imported more frequently, especially from Southeast Asia. At that time, plant lovers were most passionate about species from the *Cryptocoryne* genus: as soon as we heard that a given importer in Belgium or Holland had received a shipment of plants from Borneo or Malaysia, we hopped in our cars to see if there were any new or exciting species. Those were among my first encounters with the adult world, and certain people still remain present, such as Dr. Michel, Mr. Chichery, and Jean-François Fels. It was thanks to these imports that several new species were described for science. At that time, we were still unaware of the dangers of over-harvesting in certain biotopes, in terms of preserving the species. We were simply thrilled to receive plants directly from the riverbeds of tropical forests. It was at that time that I became aware of the adaptability of plants. In fact, these *Cryptocoryne* arrived still bearing the leaves that they had grown in the original streams. Now the physico-chemical makeup of the water and substrates, as well as the intensity and quality of the light, were obviously quite different from what one could install in an aquarium. Keep in mind that, at that time, there was very little ecological data available on the ecosystems of tropical forests, and even less on the aquatic biotopes of the forest understory. It took until the 1970s for clear and somewhat extensive data on *Cryptocoryne* ecology to become the subject of scientific writing. For example, the leaves that were then grown in aquariums (at least for those plants that survived the uprooting, storage, shipment, and transfer to new waters) were often quite different from those that were present upon arrival. The dimensions, shapes, vein patterns, blade colors – everything about these new leaves suggested a totally different species from what had initially been received. This adaptability fascinated me, and by reading an increasing number of specialized journals (particularly in German, which I barely mastered), I slowly came to understand plant reactivity and their innate faculty for adaptation. I believe that it was by observing these *Cryptocoryne* as an adolescent that I was definitively steered toward research in tropical botany.

But the vertical garden, where is its genesis? It was at around the same time, when I was fifteen, that I read an article in a German journal on how the immersed roots of plants living above the waterline could purify aquarium waters. I already understood how submerged aquatic plants would recycle the nitrates leeched from excess fish food and excrement. But I could not have imagined that aerial plants might prosper only as a result of the mineral elements accumulating in connection with fish. Of course, today we are all familiar with methods for purifying pools and polluted waters using plant lagooning techniques, but those methods were still only bubbling to the surface at the end of the 1960s. And so I was eager to take cuttings from a creeping Araceae, a "philodendron" (in fact, a *Monstera deliciosa*) that my mother was growing in the living room, in order to root them in my aquarium's filter. That filter reminded me very much of the one from our doctor's waiting room that had fascinated me ten years earlier, with the following exception: the filter in my aquarium was placed just above the waterline and not in an attached compartment. In a few weeks, I saw that the *Monstera* was thriving and sending out strong new roots into the aquarium water through the filtering layers. From then on, I understood that everything I had learned in church (I was brought up Protestant) and in school, even in high school, concerning "nourishing soil" needed to be completely revisited. And beyond breaking through the soil, I was especially fascinated by the pure white roots that the fish did not consume (though probably for the simple reason that Araceae produce several toxic compounds, such as various alkaloids and heterosides!). Whatever the case, it was around the age of fifteen that something clicked and pulled me out of the water. My love for plants and aquatic animals remains intact today, but I have moved toward the protected and moist shaded zones of the understory of tropical forests.

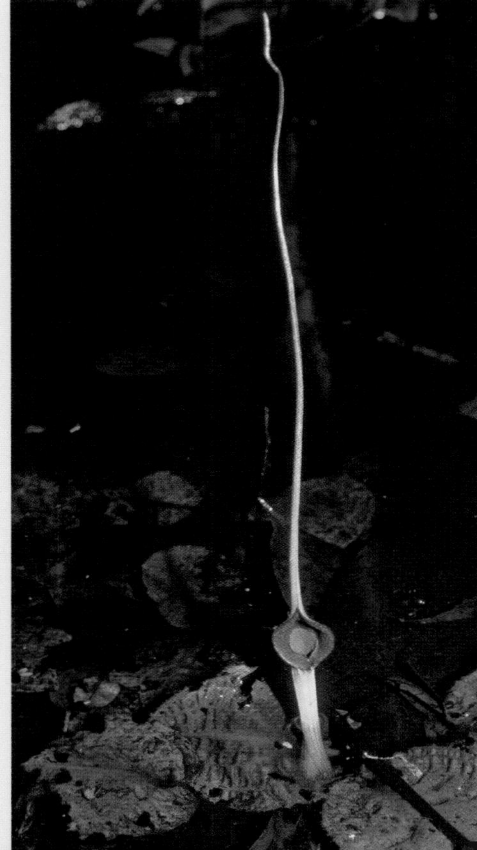

It was between the ages of fifteen and eighteen that everything fell into place. Fish still interested me as long as they could thrive in small containers. I took the large aquarium off its table and placed it on the ground, adding

October 30, 2007, day of the inauguration of the vertical gardens at the Taipei Concert Hall.

more and more species of plants whose roots pushed into the filter. A bamboo trellis about six feet high and anchored in the filter allowed the branches of my *Philodendron* and other Araceae to be supported as they grew. I grew tired of its somewhat static character and remembered the images of the waterfalls in the Bois de Boulogne and at the Paris Flower Show, as well as numerous documentaries that I had so avidly watched on television. I decided at that point to recreate a waterfall, recycling the aquarium water through the root systems of my plants. I installed a wood plank covered with a thin sheet of plastic above the aquarium. An electric pump pulled the water up and let it flow continually along a horizontal tube installed at the top of the structure. At first, the stems of these creeping plants were merely tied to the top of the plank. Water continued to flow over them, allowing new roots to sprout out of the aquarium along the structure's perpetual stream. This mechanically unstable assemblage, with its continual six-foot flow of water, was obviously the cause of a few minor catastrophes. As soon as an older *Philodendron* leaf bent under its own weight, the water would stream along the petiole and splash down onto the floor, often creating trouble for our downstairs neighbors. I nevertheless kept this far from ideal system running for a few years.

My first trip to the tropics was ultimately the revelation leading to the "invention." In 1972, I was nineteen years old and studying for my degree in the natural sciences at the University of Jussieu. Like many students I worked several evenings and Saturdays in order to earn a little money, even though my parents were still fully supporting me. I spent the majority of that pocket money at Alcazar, located across from the Samaritaine department store, where I was selling fish for aquariums. It is impossible for me not to connect that humid and protected nighttime scene, peopled by strange and talented creatures, with the images of the tropical rainforest understory that I was discovering at the same time. In the summer of 1972 I left for Thailand and Malaysia with a friend, with the intention of discovering my cherished *Cryptocoryne* in their natural habitats. (My parents were anxious and so decided to accompany me on part of the trip.) In central Thailand I discovered the tropical forest of the Khao Yai National Park. In fact, the images that are the true origin of the vertical garden date from those first sensations, when we practically hijacked a pickup truck to take us at nightfall to the center of the park. We traveled about twenty-five miles in clouds and sometimes in pouring rain, clutching the metal frame, in order to contemplate these wild visions: a *Platycerium* clinging to a forking tree one hundred feet high; *Drynaria, Davallia,* and other ferns dripping from the trunks of trees (Dipterocarpaceae, which my mother called "cement trees"); the embankments covered with herbaceous species that would later become the subject of my research (Gesneriaceae, Urticaceae, Melastomataceae, Rubiaceae, Commelinaceae ...), the smells and sounds .... In the days that followed, our forest walks along the waterfalls revealed other surprises: entire swaths of vegetation (which I later discovered were mostly *Pogonatherum* and *Elatostema*) hidden behind curtains of water while others covered the splattered rocks. The trees hanging over the waterfalls were full of epiphytes, mostly orchids, ferns, lycopods, and hoyas. Another of my great delights was to see how much the rocks in the forest understory were covered with delicate little plants with their strange silvery and brownish patterns. These were my first sightings of *Sonerila, Argostemma, Begonia, Henckelia.* From then on, I understood that plants could sprout at any height, not merely from the ground, in order to then climb. That is the difference between soil-based creepers and the epiphytes or lithophytes that colonize any favorable spot on a branch or rock, regardless of height and without ever touching the soil. It was monsoon season, so everything was luxuriant. The trampled paths of elephants left an impression without making me afraid. I was unaware that tigers were then abundant in the National Park and that several park rangers had lost their lives in accidents. As for my cherished *Cryptocoryne*, I walked along all of the forest streams and came across none. I didn't realize that they were rare in that region. The only species I ended up seeing on that first visit was growing at a sewer outlet in a Bangkok suburb! It was in fact the most common of the species (*C. ciliata*), which grows along all of the coastal regions of tropical Asia. Since then I have had the pleasure of observing several species in the forest streams of Malaysia, Sumatra, and Borneo. But that first trip to the tropics was a revelation that herbaceous and shrubby plants could colonize any available support, whether dry or soaked, in direct light or in the deepest shadows of the understory, in the most unreachable locations or along roadsides, on a lone boulder, or on the stones of temple ruins.

Back home in Suresnes, I discovered that my homemade waterfall above the aquarium was a bit paltry. I decided to expand it to the ceiling by installing a wood plank covered in sealant. I had seen how in nature plants were capable of takind hold on any support, at any height, provided there was available water. I decided to no longer simply root the plants in the aquarium, but to sprout them all along the wood plank. To that end I already had a nearly complete irrigation system, which was quite basic. It consisted of a plastic tube with holes pierced evenly throughout with a hot needle. In order to approach what I had seen in the tropical forest, I used sphagnum mosses collected from clean freshwater ponds in the area (fortunately, those mosses and the peat bogs that they create are protected today). They were held up by a grille running the length of the plank. I already had come up with the idea of affixing the grille with the staples that my mother used for hanging fabric on the apartment walls. Everything held pretty well. I made small incisions in the grille where I could position the plants, which were

mainly Araceae, Bromeliaceae, Orchidaceae, and ferns. Everything went well for a couple of months but then the sphagnum mosses subsided and decomposed, instead of growing as I had hoped. It was to be expected, since these mosses only survive in mineral-poor waters; the tap water in the Paris suburbs is hard water, high in calcium carbonate and other mineral salts. The plants that I had added remained alive since, despite the substrate falling apart, the automatic watering prevented the roots from drying out. In order to help the substrate last, I decided to use blocks of compacted peat. This helped maintain the moisture and root growth but, once again, after a few months, the substrate was disintegrating. I was far from those scenes in Khao Yai, with the centuries-old tree trunks and boulders that had persisted for several millennia! The aquarium water was also becoming rich in humic acids, greatly lowering the pH level and turning the water a strong tea color. This is common in certain understory ponds in the tropical forest, but is quite unpleasant at home.

As time passed I continued my attempts, without too many preoccupations because, in the end, everything was going well enough. My only goal was to improve the conditions so my plants could grow. The following year I returned to Malaysia and Thailand with a friend from university: new adventures, new images, and this time with complete freedom. New attempts at substrates for my plants ensued. As a good student of biology and ecology, I of course only wanted to use natural materials such as coco fiber or mineral wool, completely forgetting that whatever is biodegradable will, by definition, decompose and therefore cannot sustain a stable living environment for long. And so I tried nearly everything over the course of several months and years, consistently running into problems with weight and subsiding substrates. I finally had to admit that what I had observed in nature was a substrate only a fraction of an inch (a few millimeters) thick, often composed of a fine humus film, a thin layer of moss or a layer of algae. But in nature, those substrates are dynamic: decomposition takes place within while they reconstruct themselves on the top layer. This balance is the reason for landslides down slopes or rock faces after heavy rains. Of course, other sites, such as cave entrances, remain protected and maintain their equilibrium almost eternally (if you consider the lifespan of plants). My goal then was to replicate what I was observing in nature, while guaranteeing a certain level of long-term stability. I had no desire to see my precious plants collapse and disappear into the aquarium.

An old floor cloth covered in algae, moss, and other small plants that I found in an empty lot near the university was in fact the base for the vertical garden. I immediately saw how it connected to my observations in the tropical forest, and when I got home, I stapled a floor cloth to the plank. Since the floor cloth conducted water and held it between its fibers, I was able to cut back on watering to a few minutes every four hours. I then noticed a healthy level of root growth in my plants in a very short period of time. The only problem: floor cloths are made of cotton. Even if they partially dry out between watering they end up decomposing and releasing a terrible odor familiar to all of us. Yet I knew that the solution was at hand, since these thin fibers in contact with oxygen and light became a living support system, disappearing under algae and moss and favoring the growth of my plants' roots.

The last stage was perhaps the most decisive: I thought of using the textiles normally placed horizontally in greenhouses in order to maintain a certain humidity around the potted plants. A simple test with a lighter's flame proved that the fibers of these recycled fabrics were synthetic, and therefore rot-proof. I purchased these unwoven textiles, called "irrigation lining," to replace my cotton floor cloth. Everything was perfect. That must have been around 1977. Thirty years later, I have remained faithful to that solution and my oldest vertical garden is now twenty-five years old, even surviving a move. Since then, my work on vertical gardens has evolved, not through continued experimentation, but by approximating through observation and imagination my perpetual immersions among the world's natural environments.

Early January 2008, when finalizing the drawings for a new work, during a botanical travel in Hawaii.

1

Natural habitats

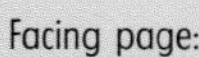

Facing page:
In northern Thailand, at the summit of Doi Inthanon, nearly 9,200 feet (2,800 m) high, are found species with purely tropical affinities, such as ferns of the *Araiostegia* genus, covering tree trunks, and other genera with temperate affinities, such as *Rhododendron* and *Hypericum*. Yet a rather surprising climbing plant takes over the bases of tree trunks in these mountaintop forests: strange Commelinaceae (the "wandering Jew"), *Streptolirion volubile*, which has perfectly heart-shaped leaves.

Summer 2007 was the time I discovered the incredible juxtaposition of dry and humid floras in the Canary Islands. Along a medium-height cliff, such as here in the Anaga mountains northeast of Tenerife, you find several moist-loving species, such as *Selaginella* and *Gesnouinia*, on a single boulder, while on the slightly more exposed faces there are *Aeonium canariense*. I was quite astonished to discover that most *Aeonium* species were perfect candidates for my vertical gardens.

Waterfalls

Waterfalls fascinate everyone, in whatever latitude they are found. In every country, they are a main tourist attraction. They provide a spot for a summer swim in temperate zones, year-round in the tropics. We can also contemplate their sculpted ice walls during winter months in colder zones. Beyond the rushing water, waterfalls are just as attractive for the lush vegetation that surrounds them. That vegetation, which is generally herbaceous and carpeting, feels calming, as the leaves undulate in the gentle winds created by the falls.

Even though they are often found in open, well-lit places, areas spattered by falls are related more to the forest understory by their flora. These permanently damp zones are colonized by understory species that are normally found along the rocky banks of streams. But unlike understory rocks, which are often quite sparsely colonized, the damp walls near waterfalls are often entirely hidden under plant life. Depending on the location, leaves are splashed with large drops of water or gently dampened by the spray, up to several hundred yards (meters) away. In some cases, water seeps over the rock surfaces, dampening only the roots. The stone surface, roots, and sometimes leaves are covered over with a sticky veil of blue algae, diatoms, and bacteria that clearly cause no harm to plant growth. Plant life is generally so dense that it forms a vertical carpet from the top of the falls to the bottom.

These favorable growing conditions, with water constantly available and natural light stronger than in the understory result in dynamic reproduction, both through sexual and vegatitive means (stolons). This allows for rapid growth outward from wherever a seed takes hold, so much so that there is often competition between the various species. Bearing witness to this competition, there are generally only three or four species around any given waterfall. From one site to the next in a geographic region, various species may come to occupy these habitats, proof of their capacity for colonization once a seed takes root. Chance plays quite a major role, since several species appear interchangeable. It thus appears that sites highly favorable to plant growth are much less favorable to botanical diversity. These sites are often quite unstable and whole areas of the vegetation may often collapse, leaving patches of bare substrate that are quickly recolonized.

The lush herbaceous species belong mostly to the genera *Asplundia*, *Begonia*, *Besleria*, *Pilea*, and *Pitcairnia* in America to *Begonia*, *Brillantaisia*, *Impatiens*, and *Elatostema* in Africa and Madagascar, and to *Begonia*, *Curculigo*, *Colocasia*, *Cyrtandra*, *Elatostema*, *Homalomena*, and *Impatiens* in Asia. Pteridophytes, most notably *Selaginella*, can be found in abundance on the three continents. In temperate Eurasia and North America diversity is lower among local species along waterfalls, yet some are nonetheless remarkable, such as *Acorus gramineus* or various *Chrysosplenium* species.

Facing page:
In Cuba's forested limestone hills, many waterfalls are covered with plants. One of the most spectacular, *Begonia nelumbifolia*, an alien species originating in Mexico, bears huge oval leaves that hang downwards. Most of the waterfalls are lined with *Russelia equisetiformis* (which is probably also an alien species), growing in extremely moist conditions–against the general opinion of most of the Riviera's growers of this species.

Waterfalls

1 - Waterfalls in the temperate zones have no reason to envy those in more tropical regions in terms of how plants cover the rocks. Here, in the Welsh countryside, besides several *Carex* and *Agrostis stolonifera* (which also covers my Chaumont waterfall), you find a wonderful little Saxifragaceae with succulent leaves, *Chrysosplenium oppositifolium*, specialized in the colonization of emergent boulders in rapids and waterfalls. *Anagallis tenella*, a minuscule pimpernel reminiscent of *Helxine*, grows along the moist slopes.

2 - Fortunately there still remain a few unspoiled locations in Java, despite a very dense human population. In the mountain forests on the Gunung Gede volcano, just above the city of Bogor, waterfalls and hot springs allow a number of species to thrive, both on the boulders of the waterfall and on the trunk and branches of the trees that are bathed in the intensely humid atmosphere.

3 - The waterfalls at Doi Inthanon in northern Thailand are spectacular during the rainy season, the monsoon that falls from June to October. Curtains of water veil a dense carpet of plants, a few inches behind it, essentially made of *Colocasia*, several species of *Elatostema* and a small, bamboo-like Gramineae, *Pogonatherum paniceum*. This *Pogonatherum* is probably the most frequently observed plant along Asian waterfalls, from India to New Guinea. It's easy to see why this species, which is routinely sold as a houseplant, dries out so rapidly when one forgets to water it. It is clearly one of the best candidates for any vertical gardens recreating a waterfall.

1

2

3

1

2

3

4

5

6

7

1 - In the Erawan National Park, in western Thailand, the last of a series of seven waterfalls offers an amazing spectacle resulting from the processes of limestone and sediment dissolution and deposit, all incrusted with algae and moss. In fact, as in the case of the well-known stromatoliths that represent the first traces of life on earth, these giant cones are made of an intricate blending of plant and mineral elements. *Pogonatherum, Elatostema,* and *Adiantum* colonize the main water course.

2 - Along the vertical rock walls of this waterfall on Gunung Gede in Java, *Elatostema* colonizes the rock by spreading out laterally along stems that are tightly attached to the rock. The rocky walls covered in plants are only inches removed from the falls themselves and are watered consistently by the spray.

3 - Certain ferns, especially the *Trichomanes* species have a preference for water-splattered rocks, like here at Doi Suthep, in northern Thailand.

4 - Also at Doi Suthep the boulders of another waterfall are covered by some large-leaf form of *Acorus gramineus,* often called *A. tatarinowii.* This species, whose distribution is centered on China and Japan, underlines again the temperate affinities of northern Thailand's mountain flora. Along with *Agrostis stolonifera,* this small *Acorus* is one of the rare species perfectly adapted to vertical gardens' waterfalls in the Parisian climate.

5 - *Ixora* are small shrubs of the Rubiaceae family and several *I. coccinea* hybrids are cultivated in tropical gardens for their beautiful orange or red tubular flowers. Several species of *Ixora* grow on rocks along waterfalls and are rheophytes, which means that they are regularly submerged during flooding, as here in eastern Thailand.

6 - This *Impatiens* growing on the rocks of a waterfall in Sikkim seems to be *I. mengtzeana,* displaying its superb orangey-beige flowers. In this particular station, the permanently wet leaves are covered over with a sticky film, made up mostly of bacteria and diatoms. Numerous species of *Impatiens* are confined to waterfalls in Madagascar as well as in Africa and Asia.

7 - The rocks of this waterfall in the hills at the northern tip of the Andes, in Venezuela, are covered with mosses and different species of *Adiantum, Peperomia, Begonia,* and *Pilea.* But the most remarkable species is a *Dicranopygium,* from the Cyclanthaceae family, which is endemic to tropical America. Most *Dicranopygium* grow around waterfalls and have long, split leaves that better resist the water current or broader leaves, reminiscent of palm leaves, that tend to tear at the edges without affecting their growth, like the wind-shredded banana leaves.

1 - In the mountains of the Canary Islands the humid forests are full of seeping rocks and small waterfalls. This one, on La Gomera, is covered by an enormous fern, *Woodwardia radicans,* and by *Gesnouinia arborea,* a shrub of the Urticaceae family that is oddly reminiscent of the *Debregeasia* found in eastern Africa and Asia. Among the small succulent plants adapted to this wet biotope, it is surprising to find a species from the xerophilous family of Crassulaceae, *Aichryson pachycaulon,* the *Aichryson* genus having mainly evolved by splitting into different species in these islands' humid and shaded biotopes.

2 - The famous Ekom falls in Cameroon served as a natural backdrop for the filming of *Greystoke: The Legend of Tarzan.* Thanks to the spray that the falls produce year-round, even in the dry season, relict fragments of dense humid forest have survived in the midst of an area currently characterized by savannas.

3 - On the slopes and rocky outcrops near the Ekom falls, the herbaceous relict forest species survive, such as several *Anubias, Crinum,* and *Begonia,* including the splendid *B. poculifera* with its bright yellow flowers. But in areas exposed to sunlight, the landscape is largely dominated by *Impatiens irvingii,* covered with pink flowers and over 3 feet (1 m) in height.

4 - The Carbet falls in Guadeloupe are one of the island's main tourist attractions. On both sides of the waterfall the spray on the cliff face encourages the growth of several species of *Pilea* and *Peperomia,* as well as the Bromeliaceae *Pitcairnia angustifolia,* the Cyclantaceae *Asplundia insignis* and *A. rigida,* and even the Araceae *Philodendron giganteum* with its large orbicular leaves.

1

2

3

Riverbanks

The banks along rivers and streams are often characterized by an unstable substrate eroding in various ways depending on its mineralogical makeup as well as on the direction and strength of the water. Several species grow on the relatively stable vertical banks and on overhanging ledges, both in temperate and tropical regions. Their roots colonize the top layer, whether rock or soil. The plants multiply through runners, suckers, and basal sprouts, allowing the plants to resist being torn away by erosion. They also fight erosion itself with their dense and intricate root systems. Plants growing along river banks are called "ripicolous." Certain species may grow just as easily in forests, on rocks or along banks, while others are strictly ripicolous. Many ferns can be found both on rocks and along river banks. On the other hand, larger-seeded plants may grow on river banks but will not germinate on rocks. If the bank slopes very gradually, the area may be regularly flooded and become a low-lying swampy area.

Rocks that protrude up to some inches above the waterline are always moist because the carpet of moss helps to carry water over the rock through capillary action. After each heavy rainfall, the rocks are immersed in rapid-flowing waters. Those plants that anchor themselves to the substrates and are regularly washed by the water flow are called rheophytes (*rheos* means "flow" in Greek). The various rheophyte species share several morphological and behavioral characteristics, most notably the presence of tough, elongated leaves, short or "carpeting" stems, a thick and dense root system covering and slightly disintegrating the rocks, small seeds and seedlings capable of taking hold in the smallest cracks or in the wet moss when the water level is low. Emerging rheophytes may also be found in open places in temperate regions. Many species of willow and oleander are good examples of this. In tropical regions rheophytes number many species, including trees and shrubs as well as herbaceous species.

Most herbaceous or poorly lignified vines grow on trees along the forest edge or on vast metallic structures that lie abandoned. The most common belong to Convolvulaceae, Cucurbitaceae, and Vitaceae. Once the stems reach the top of an available support structure, they hang like broad drapes, like a single-species vertical garden, as is the case with this *Turbina corymbosa* that, like a giant bat, covers a partially dead tree along the banks of a river in Ecuador.

Facing page:
The genus *Aglaonema* spreads across all of Southeast Asia, and even though it only numbers about twenty species, it is found almost everywhere. Certain species grow on the forest floor, others take to karstic outcrops, enduring long periods of drought, while still others grow on the rocks and banks of streams, such as here in southern Thailand. As a general rule these plants are perfect for the lower sections of vertical gardens.

1 - The different species of the great genus *Pandanus* (more than 700 species!) are very difficult to identify. In fact these plants rarely flower and are dioecious, meaning the male and female flowers are produced by different plants. Collecting samples is a delicate maneuver because of their often immense leaves lined with sharp thorns. Most habitats harbor several different species, especially in Asia and Madagascar. A few species live along beaches, while others prefer seaside cliffs, or inselbergs, mountain forests, lowland forest understories, swampy forests, or the banks of forest, swampy woods, or the edge of forest streams like this small species in Sumatra, *Pandanus pentodon*, capable of obstructing the river bed as its spreads out through basal suckers.

2 - Also in Sumatra, though this photograph could have been taken in many other regions of Southeast Asia, the fern *Microsorum pteropus* grows among the rocks and on the banks of fast-flowing forest streams, firmly anchored by a rhizome with roots that take hold in the smallest cracks in the rock. This species is well known to aquarium hobbyists because it also develops very well under water.

3 - The streams of the humid tropical forests are only a few inches or a few dozen inches deep, with little variation between the rainy and dry season. The trees and shrubs that grow along the banks send out many branching roots to capture water and mineral salts present in low concentrations. You also find this type of roots in the pool at the base of a vertical garden, coming from plants installed at its top.

4 - Small, red *Ardisia crenata* berries are consumed by birds which then disperse the seeds from their perches above the riverbanks. Here, in the famous Kokedera moss garden in Kyoto, *Ardisia* is the only shrub that the gardeners allow to root among the moss, perhaps because its red berries are believed to bring wealth and happiness. At its base, a tuft of *Heloniopsis orientalis* grows just along the edge. This species is usually confined to the vertical slopes in the forest understory.

5 & 6 - It might be considered heresy to grow oleander along highway slopes subject to long droughts, especially when one is aware that, in nature, this species normally grows along the banks of fast-flowing rivers, as here on a small mountain north of Valencia, Spain. In fact it deals well with drought since even in its natural habitat rivers often dry up for several months at a time, like wadis. But the most beautiful populations of oleanders occur along permanent streams, as here. Their long, white roots branch out to form a vast underwater mattress, and each individual plant has multiple trunks, making them potentially immortal. Their long, tough leaves are characteristic of most rheophytic shrubs, adapted to fast-flowing streams.

1

2

3

4

5

6

1

2

1 - *Rotula aquatica,* of the Boraginaceae family, is a tropical species typical of rivers with highly variable water flow and low-altitude streams with strong currents. It can be found in America, Africa, and Asia. It grows on rocks and between pebbles in the riverbed. Its leaves and flowers are visible in the dry season, when the water levels recede, as here in the month of February in Mali.

2 - The banks of the Amazonian rivers are usually covered with herbaceous and climbing plants, making access difficult. On the banks of the Rio Villano, in Ecuador, frequently submerged boulders are covered with *Cuphea bombonasae* which spreads out in lateral stems that cling to the rock by adventitious roots, while the embankment slopes are covered with several species of *Philodendron,* ferns, *Psychotria,* and Vitaceae vines. One of the most remarkable species along the Ecuadorian riverbanks is *Carludovica palmata,* the famous Cyclanthaceae whose young palmate leaves are used for making Panama hats (keep in mind that the origin of the craft is in Ecuador and not in Panama).

3 - The banks of forest rivers in the eastern United States are often covered with *Leucothoe fontanesiana,* a shrub with arching branches of the Ericaceae family. When these *Leucothoe* are planted horizontally in a garden, the branch ends die off gloomily when reaching the ground. Only when they are supported obliquely or vertically can they grow as they would in nature, as here in the state of Georgia.

4 - In Venezuela's Gran Sabana, at the foot of the Kukenan *tepui,* the natural vegetation is a mosaic of forest and savanna. Along the edges of the forest blocks, streams welcome numerous submerged and emerging species, such as this *Cassia* (Cesalpiniaceae) growing on the bank, whose branches spread horizontally just above the water's surface, offering its bright yellow flowers to pollinators.

5 - A few yards from this *Cassia,* in the same stream in the Gran Sabana, a small tree of the genus *Tabebuia* (Bignoniaceae) shows off the typical traits of rheophyte shrubs, repeatedly exposed to the force of the currents. Starting with a stump anchored firmly in the ground, multiple stems displaying tough elongate foliate leaves bend in the direction of the current.

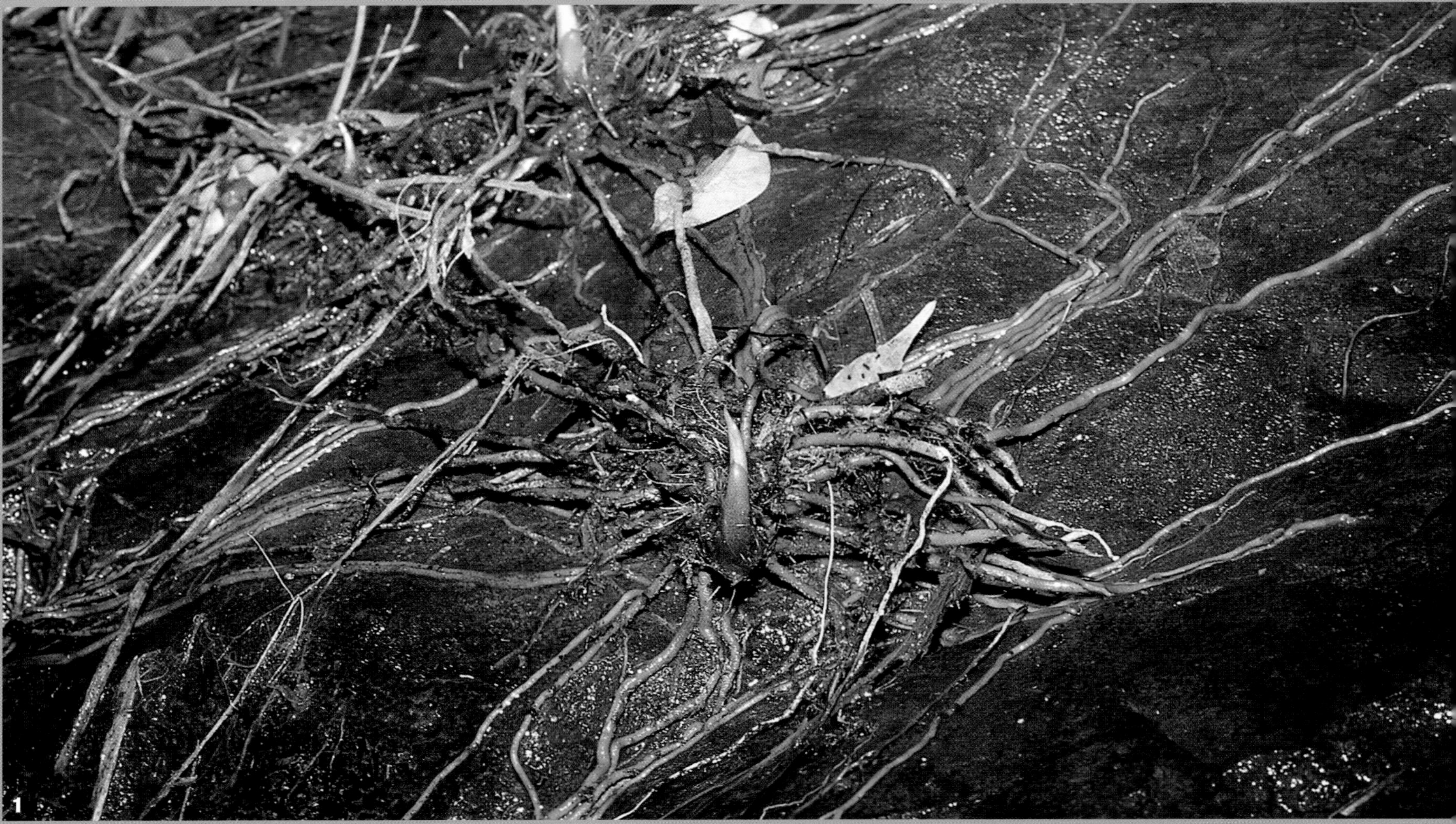

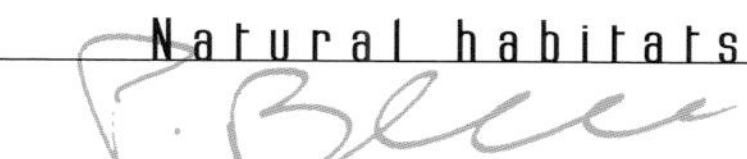

Seeping rocks

1 & **2** - What a curious idea it is to cultivate *Hosta* in horizontal beds in the gardens! In nature, primarily in Japan, as seen here on Kyushu Island, different species of *Hosta* typically grow on the wet rocks bordering waterfalls. Their superficial root system radiates outward in the film of algae covering the rock, from the plant base, which is perfectly visible here, toward the end of winter, before new leaves cover up the root system. Growth conditions in nature are therefore quite similar to those of the vertical garden: the irrigation cloth is comparable to an algae bed, and the PVC reproduces the rock's rigidity.

3 - On this wet rock face in the Khao Yai National Park, northeast of Bangkok, the roots of *Begonia, Boesenbergia, Globba,* and other *Elatostema* intermingle with the roots of shrubs and trees that provide them with the shade they need. During the dry season, the root ends die off, promoting the development of secondary roots at the onset of the rainy season, thus increasing the total surface area of the root system for nutrient absorption and adherence to the substrate.

4 - Little known by plant lovers and most botanists, *Homalomena* (Araceae) with its 150 species is nonetheless abundant in the forest understory of Southeast Asia. Rarely does one walk 50 yards (meters) in the forest without encountering some species of *Homalomena* on a slope, a wet rock, or a riverbank, like here in the forest understory of eastern Thailand.

5 - Numerous species of *Phyllanthus* are confined to wet rocks and edges of waterfalls. This very speciose genus of the *Euphorbiaceae* family (nearly 600 species) is found in a variety of biotopes in tropical regions. Many species resemble ferns, but a closer inspection under the leafing branches reveals the presence of small flowers. Here is another vast genus that is largely unknown to horticulture, although several species would be perfectly suited to private apartments. The shape of this unidentified species growing on the wet rocks of Koh Chang Island in eastern Thailand is reminiscent of *Phyllanthus pulcher,* which is currently developing very well on the plant columns of Bangkok's Esplanade.

6 - On another wet rock on Kyushu Island in southern Japan, *Hosta* are sprouting new leaves in early spring. On this same rock, between the *Hosta,* grows the Gesneriaceae *Conandron ramondioides,* which is particular to dripping vertical surfaces. It is most often found as a single hanging oval leaf.

Cliffs and karstic outcrops

The limestone outcrops with vertical faces rising several hundred feet above the surrounding landscape are typical of certain areas of northwestern Venezuela, northeastern Tanzania, Madagascar's *tsingies,* Along Bay in Vietnam, southern Thailand, Malaysia, Sumatra, and Borneo. These limestone areas are most extensive in Asia. They are what is left of an enormous coral reef that existed in the Primary Era (Carboniferous and Permian Periods), stretching from China (including the famous Gulin region) to Borneo, about five times the length of Australia's Great Barrier Reef. After disappearing beneath sediment, it resurfaced in the Tertiary Era when India collided with continental Asia, and was strongly eroded during the Quaternary Era as the climate and seas fluctuated. The extent and fragmentation of these karstic reliefs along a latitude gradient across Asia explains why so many plants evolved separately into endemic species on this particular substrate. In other regions, limestone formations are more spread out and worn, as in Cuba and Guadeloupe, also the remnants of former coral reefs.

On this type of substrate, the flora is extremely rich, considering that along the Malaysian peninsula around 1,200 species of vascular plants are confined to these locations, about 14 percent of the country's species, whereas the limestone formations make up only 0.3 percent of the territory. Many species are small trees and creepers. Among the herbaceous and shrubby plants, there are many Gesneriaceae, but often of different genera than those that colonize crystalline or lateritic rocks: *Boea, Paraboea, Monophyllaea, Chirita.* Various Acanthaceae are also present, most notably *Justicia* and certain *Strobilanthes* (this huge genus is, however, more typical of mountain forests). *Begonia, Impatiens, Argyreia, Argostemma, Pilea, Boesenbergia, Amorphophallus, Colocasia, Alocasia,* and *Malaxis* often occur on these limestone rocks. In Guadeloupe, several *Peperomia* and shrubby *Piper* dot the strange landscapes created by the white rocks in the understory.

Differences in structure and solubility are the reason for the sometimes razor-sharp cuts in the limestone walls and cave formations. Along the top ridges, innumerable cavities of various dimensions accumlate humus and water, with the humus often acting as a sponge. These areas are covered by more or less continuous forest, whose flora is comparable to that found in nearby forests at the foot of the outcrop. In the humid tropics, soluble calcium salts are dissolved and leached away over time. The humus is usually acidic and the plant species present are not the calcicolus species that thrive on high concentrations of calcium salts. Along the karst walls, cracks invite the accumulation of organic matter, decomposing and creating a sort of hanging "flower pot." Their size ranges from fractions of an inch to several feet in depth. The smaller plants, which either colonize the small pockets of humus or grow directly on the rock surface, experience higher concentrations of calcium salts and are mainly calcicolous. And so with only a few inches between them, calcicolous and calcifugous species grow side by side. These limestone formations often have nearly vertical walls with few tall trees, to the point that the exposure to direct light along the rocky surface is much higher than in the understory of the forest. The stronger light intensity, along with the permeability of the rock, enhances the effect of the dry season, even along the equator. The plants that grow on these karstic formations reveal various means for adapting to the drier conditions, whether through succulent stems or leaves, thick cuticles to reduce transpiration, deciduous foliage, the tuberization of stems,

Numerous shrubs and herbaceous species grow in the crevices of these limestone rocks, as here in Khao Sok. Certain smaller bamboos are common, notably *Dendrocalamus dumosus* and *D. elegans.*

Facing page:
The famous outcrop of the Phang Nga Bay in southern Thailand is part of a karstic massif similar to the one in the Along Bay, 930 miles (1,500 km) northeast of Phang Nga. Halfway there, along the Thai peninsula, other remarkable karst formations are to be found, notably in Khao Sok and Khao Sam Roi Yot. Thanks to erosion's differential wear on this limestone created from coral reefs of the Paleozoic Era, numerous cavities of various sizes and shapes occur naturally, allowing for a buildup of humus favorable to tree growth.

shortened cycle (annual behavior), or dessication tolerant foliage. Many species belonging to families and genera that are characteristic of the forest understory have evolved towards tolerance to sun-drenched, water-poor environments, such as Gesneriaceae, Urticaceae, *Impatiens*, and *Begonia*. Yet the karstic landscape is characterized by a mosaic of microhabitats. With water flow determined by differential rock erosion, there are numerous cavities that collect water and distribute it over time, even during the dry season. Along the near-permanent seeping, hygrophilous species prosper, inches away from some xerophytes on a bit of exposed, dry rock. This range of habitats on such a reduced surface is the reason for the phenomenal biodiversity of these environments.

Many species confined to karstic habitats produce small, capsular fruits. Their seeds fall within close range of the mother plant. This strategy allows plants to fully occupy, through sexual reproduction, the favorable micro-habitat they have happened to reach. Contrary to common opinion, colonizing a favorable site can take place through sexual reproduction rather than by vegetative propagation (such as by stolons). A population can thus become established from a single individual, and evolution continues through genetic drift, exchanges with other populations being often nonexistent because of the short seed dispersal distance. Only by accident – when seeds are transported along with other matter by an animal or during cyclones, for example – may new, isolated populations establish, which may in time evolve into a new species. This type of evolution through the genetic drift of small, isolated populations is reminiscent of evolutionary processes on islands, and the rate of endemism is usually very high among the smaller species of karstic habitats.

Limestone cliffs constitute a refuge for many highly endemic species. The way in which these habitats are currently receding with the development of cement-producing quarries should raise the highest concern.

As surprising as it may seem, this *Cycas tropophylla* was only described in 2004, even though it covers the cliffs that welcome tourist ships in Along Bay. For a long time botanists neglected these plants growing on karstic outcrops in the sea, assuming they were common species that had migrated from the nearby coastline. They didn't realize that these islands constitute a set of isolated microhabitats on which species have evolved through genetic drift. That is also the reason why the large and spectacular palm tree *Livistona halongensis* was only "discovered" in 1999, much like the Zingiberaceae *Alpinia calcicola* or the Gesneriaceae *Chirita hiepii* and *C. gemella*.

This other rock in Phang Nga Bay displays a fairly even topography. Small cavities occupy its entire surface, allowing trees to grow into a veritable hanging forest.

Facing page:
The natural vertical garden visible at the base of this limestone cliff near Ipoh in Malaysia is protected, while sides are covered in graffiti. The paint sticks only on the dry part of the rock, while the permanently wet section in the middle prevents the paint from drying. Besides some young Gesneriaceae (probably *Chirita* or the common *Epithema saxatile*) notice the extremely beautiful form of *Begonia kingiana*, whose brown leaves are stunningly highlighted by the bright green veins. This *Begonia*, like other species that grow on karst formations, is obviously well suited to vertical gardens that are given a regular stream of limestone-rich water.

Cliffs and karstic outcrops

1 - In Along Bay in Vietnam, this vertical limestone cliff is covered with different species, including the remarkable *Dracaena cambodiana,* with its multiple woody stems ascending to 10 or 13 feet (3 or 4 m) high, with the flexible leaves grouped at the top.

2 - Among the *Piper, Poikilospermum, Nephrolepis,* and other species, one can see the perfectly structured triangular leaves of the *Alocasia lowii* on this vertical limestone cliff in the Batu Caves near Kuala Lumpur in Malaysia. Numerous species of *Alocasia* grow in this way along the base or shady sections of karst formations throughout tropical Asia. Very few species are currently being cultivated, even in botanical gardens.

3 - A group of rocks in Along Bay, seen from the summit of one of the 2,000 islands. Most reach a height of 150 to 350 feet (50 to 100 m). The vegetation density is obviously connected to the topography, the erosion processes, and the solubility of the limestone. These karstic outcrops, created from the limestone deposits of the great barrier coral reefs at the end of the Paleozoic Era, emerged primarily with the rise of the Himalayas in the Tertiary period.

4 - This *Asparagus* has settled in a rock crevice on an island in Along Bay. Both in Asia and Africa, most species of *Asparagus* grow on vertical rock faces, which is why their stems hang down.

5 - On the same island, an *Alocasia* from the group *A. macrorrhizos* grows in a rocky crevice in a relatively open forest understory. Other Araceae, especially *Aglaonema* and *Amorphophallus,* also colonize these fissures. All produce small berries ¼ to ⅓ inch (7 to 10 mm) in diameter, containing a single large seed. Their bright red color attracts the fruit-eating birds of these karst reliefs; they eat the berries and eventually drop the seeds from their perches in the trees and shrubs into the underlying fisured rocks favorable to seed germination.

6 - A few yards away, another boulder is covered by *Pothos* from the group of *P. scandens.* This herbaceous vine from the Araceae family has roots that penetrate the rock's smallest cracks, filled with humus.

7 - In the understory of these low forests on an island in Along Bay, *Alocasia can be seen* among the rocks, as well as the common *Begonia boisiana, Hoya, Aglaonema, Aspidistra,* and even the splendid orchid *Ludisia discolor,* one of my favorite plants for the base of a vertical garden. A foray into this understory allows us to understand the extremely long-term stability of these plant formations (as long as humans don't destroy them). This *Dracaena cambodiana* is potentially immortal since from its base anchored in the rocks, new shoots are developed as older stems reaching 13 to 16 feet (4 to 5 m) high gradually lose their leaves and dry out. For these plants, death is not unavoidable, merely accidental. They will only die if confronted with long periods of drought, forest fires, or destructive human action. Judging from the numerous stems along its base, this *Dracaena* is at least several centuries old; since older stems decompose progressively, it may even be thousands of years old.

1

2

3
4
5
6
7

4

1 - These limestone cliffs in Bako National Park in Borneo are covered with *Pandanus* – among other species – on the vertical faces, while the summit is dominated by a forest of the elegantly architectured *Casuarina (Gymnostoma) nobilis.* This national park harbors a highly diverse vegetation, and plant biodiversity here is extremely high for such a small surface area.

2 - At the entrance to the Batu Caves in Malaysia certain alien species have invaded the fully exposed limestone rocks, like this *Rhoeo (Tradescantia) spathacea,* native to Mexico. *Rhoeo* seems mostly to colonize rocky micro-sites unexploited by any indigenous species. Perhaps this is due to the fact that the year-round humidity in Malaysia has prevented species from adapting to sites that are more exposed, and therefore very dry as soon as the rain stops for a couple of days. On the other hand, Mexico's climate, with its long dry season, forced plants like *Rhoeo* to adapt to seasonal droughts.

3 - In the Macaronesian isles, such as the island of La Gomera in the Canaries, the family Crassulaceae has remarkably diversified, notably in the genera *Aeonium, Greenovia,* and *Aichryson.* Most of these species colonize the vertical faces of rocks of various mineralogical compositions. This *Greenovia aurea* is found at low altitudes, yet it also colonizes rocks at altitudes up to 6,500 feet (2,000 m). Its leaves form an erect nosette, with the older, dried out leaves still visible at the edges, protecting the center from the drought and the cold.

4 - Below this cliff on one of the islands in Along Bay, tourist boats stop, with no explanation from the guides that this most common plant, *Cycas tropophylla,* was only described in 2004. Yet this kind of information can help any citizen understand the vulnerability of natural habitats and the urgent need to protect them. Not visible in this image because of their small size, the splendid *Chirita drakei* (Gesneriaceae), also indigenous to Along Bay, covers numerous crags in the rocks with their silvery leaves and blue flowers.

5 - A limestone cliff in Gunung Mulu National Park in Borneo: from 325 feet (100 m) away, from the other side of the river, one can only make out the hanging fronds of a *Nephrolepis* fern (probably *N. acutifolia*), a few *Paraboea* rosettes (Gesneriaceae), and numerous trees and shrubs. One would need to get closer to discover the *Begonia, Elatostema, Piper, Homalomena, Chirita,* and *Monophyllaea* growing on the shaded basal parts of the cliff.

Inselbergs and rocky outcrops

Steep rocky outcrops share common characteristics regardless of their location or the mineral composition of the rock. Vegetation tends to remain sparse; plants only settle into cracks or wherever there is an accumulation of humus and water. When the rock is stable, plants can become remarkably old. For example, along the Niagara's cliffs, some *Thuya occidentalis* reach 1,800 years old on the stable dolomite faces, but only 250 years old on the disintegrating schist. The weathering is both physical (strong winds, alternating freezes and thaws in temperate zones, or high daytime temperatures and cool nocturnal temperatures in tropical zones) and chemical – as precipitation differentially dissolves the mother rock.

Crystalline rocks exhibit even surfaces slightly rough to the touch. Here vascular plants only settle in cracks or on areas that are not as steep, where humus accumulates. On the other hand, volcanic rock, with its pockmarked structure, is often entirely covered with vegetation, even on vertical walls when the climate remains sufficiently humid, such as on Hawai'i's plicated cliffs. Sometimes you find exposed laterite slabs on the surface, creating oblique surfaces where there is sufficient slope (between 40 and 50 degrees). Laterite slabs and blocks often have an uneven surface, offering cavities that trap water and humus. Steep smooth rocky surfaces, such as most granites and sandstones, remain bare. In more open areas they are sometimes covered in algae, Cyanophyceae, and lichens; in more humid understory they may also be covered with mosses, hepatics, ferns, and flowering plants. Different terms are used to describe plants restricted to rocky areas, such as "saxicolous," "rupicolous," "epilithic," or "lithophytic." I will stick with "saxicolous," the term most commonly used.

Even in sub-desert regions, rocky outcrops are often home to shrubby and arborescent vegetation. This is caused by a combination of biological and microclimatic factors. Difficult access prevents grazing wildlife from reaching the plants, as can easily be seen in the East African savannas where the only wooded areas occur on inselbergs and smaller rocky outcrops, or clusters of broad boulders. Barren rock surface protects the vegetation from bush fires. Temperature fluctuations are higher on the rock surface than within the plant formations, and heavy dew collects over the course of the night as the rock cools down. The dew creates small flowing channels that offer moisture for plants to grow, even without rain. You often find these damp or even seeping rock walls in forests even if it has not rained for many days and the forest soil has dried out. Rocky walls at the base of inselbergs, such as at the Nouragues research camp, continue to produce a trickle of water even at the peak of the dry season, because of the large collecting surface area.

Species that are restricted to these rocky massifs have often adapted to tolerate droughts. This is evident in succulent leaves and stems, as with *Agave*, *Echeveria*, *Dyckia*, and most Cactaceae in tropical America or with *Aloe*, *Euphorbia*, and numerous Crassulaceae, Compositae, Aizoaceae, and Asclepiadaceae in Africa and Madagascar, and even with *Sedum*, *Sempervivum*, some *Androsace*, and *Saxifraga* in Europe.

In the case of trees and shrubs without any apparent adaptive morphology to fluctuating levels of water and temperatures, the plants change their growth habits to adjust to the conditions of the biotope: apex

Even though it is not strictly confined to rocky massifs, *Lindera obtusiloba* (Lauraceae) is a small understory tree that frequently grows on slopes. The perfect architecture of its leaves and the butter-yellow color that they take on in autumn make them one of the most remarkable elements of the temperate forest understories of the Far East, like here in the mountains west of Tokyo.

Facing page:
A twenty-minute taxi ride from central Seoul, in South Korea, is all it takes to find yourself in the midst of Bukhansan National Park. The rock disintegrating in broad slabs welcomes several plant species in its many cracks, for example *Rhododendron mucronulatum,* which flowers in early spring. A closer examination would reveal the stunning *Mukdenia rossii,* a Saxifragaceae whose rhizomes colonize the exposed surface of the rock where water trickles in the spring as the snows melt.

development of the stems takes place during the rainy season, then the tips die off during the dry season. This triggers the development of two to three new branches just below the dead apex at the onset of the following rainy season. The process produces a very dense crown not unlike the crowns of the tropical rainforest trees, as I was able to point out during my observations from the canopy raft. In the case of species with flexuous and arching shoots, like many *Cotoneaster, Berberis, Escallonia, Baccharis, Buddleja, Coriaria, Hypericum, Philadelphus,* sub-apex ramification is less pronounced and only clearly visible in one or two of the main axes. This arched shape, typical of many shrubs of steep slopes in temperate climate, withstands better the weight of the snow in winter and allows it to slide off. This also represents a remarkable adaptation for optimizing exposure to direct and indirect sunlight since the diagonal rays hitting temperate zones reach the foliage perpendicularly. Moreover, these flexuous stems, weighted down as they reach between 3 and 6 feet (1 and 3 m) in length, depending on the species, produce new basal shoots similar to those existing. From an initial plant, these shrubs spread out by creating new stems that then take root and become more independent plants. This has two important biological consequences: first, these shrubs are resistant to uprooting in storms or rock slides because the plants' center of gravity is so close to the rock surface and the root system is so extensively fortified; second, the repetitive basal ramification practically guarantees the plant's immortality.

Regardless of the latitude or composition of the rock, inselbergs and other rocky outcrops are home to many highly endemic species. Thirty-five to forty percent of species that are endemic to the Alps are strictly confined to crevices and fissures in steep rocky slopes. The rate reaches 65 percent in New Zealand. In Eurasia, these are the original habitat of many species of *Saxifraga, Draba, Sorbus, Daphne, Dianthus, Campanula, Androsace, Corydalis, Rhododendron,* and others. The overexploitation of the natural stations of numerous species of *Rhododendron* confined to these rocky habitats in China, Japan, and the Himalayas, over the twentieth century has resulted in the extinction of several species. Similarly, natural bonsai's – the result of repeated branch tip dieback and drying-up of whole sections of branches directly due to the plant's position in exposed rocks – have nearly disappeared from Japan's landscapes, as a result of over-harvesting during the last two centuries. In tropical regions, granite and sandstone inselbergs are not as intensively quarried as karstic areas.

The sensual, rocky domes of the inselbergs near our CNRS research station at the Nouragues camp in French Guiana. These very ancient granite rocks have only slowly eroded and my colleague Corine Sarthou has pointed out the processes of plant succession colonizing the bare rock. First, different species of blue algae (Cyanophyceae) take hold and create a microlayer of humus, which then welcomes other species such as green algae, moss, and hepatics, and then finally, Angiosperms (flowering plants). Among the dominant shrubs that are clearly visible in the image are *Clusia* and several species of Myrtaceae.

Facing page:
At the base of the granite boulders of the Nouragues inselberg is a Convolvulaceae that is apparently endemic to French Guiana, *Ipomoea leprieurii.* I was able to show that this species is remarkable for its capacity to adjust its behavior according to its habitat. In very exposed areas with strong vertical drainage, the species is annual, since it dies from dehydration in the dry season, whereas at the foot of the rock faces, it survives because the rhizomes do not dry up. Under rock faces, stone fragments trap the humus and the water collected from nighttime condensation on the rock, which occurs even in the dry season. At the beginning of the rainy season, the plants that develop from the rhizomes are the first to flower, while those that come from seed develop and blossom later. This double strategy in a single species – one based on an early death brought on by the establishment site, the other based on potential immortality – allows the species to extend its growth, flowering, and seed dispersion cycles over a longer period of time.

At an altitude of more than 8,200 feet (2,500 m), the Kukenan *tepui* towers high above Venezuela's Gran Sabana. On these isolated massifs, strong winds prevent the establishment of high forests. Low forests dominated by *Bonnetia roraimae* (from a family close to Theaceae) grow in only the most protected of sites. The wind also prevents humus from accumulating, and this absence of organic matter probably promoted the establishment of several species of carnivorous plants capable of digesting nitrogen from trapped insects. The most common genera of carnivorous plants along the barren rocks of these *tepuis* are *Utricularia, Drosera,* and the endemic genus *Heliamphora.* Even among the Bromeliaceae, a few species evolved into carnivores, such as this *Brocchinia reducta* (whose shape and color are reminiscent of *Greenovia aurea* in the Canary Islands). In the case of the *Brocchinia,* insects often don't fall to the bottom of the tube formed by its overlapping leaves. Spiders spin their webs and settle in the middle to trap insects sliding along the vertical tube of leaves.

1

2

3

4

5

6

7

1 - The rock faces, bathed in the nightly mists along the summit of the Soufrière volcano in Guadeloupe, are covered by a thick layer of moss. It is among this moss that angiosperm seeds germinate, notably from Bromeliaceae of the genera *Pitcairnia* and *Glomeropitcairnia*, along with *Philodendron giganteum* and *Asplundia rigida* in the more sheltered spots. The moss develops on its periphery, with no root system, letting its lower part die and decompose into humus, where the roots of the Angiosperms find their nutrients. With heavy rain, entire sections of moss break off and the plant succession starts anew on the barren rock.

2 - An unevenly eroded summit of an isolated rocky outcrop completely covered by vegetation usually indicates a limestone base, as here in Khao Sok, in southern Thailand. Granite or sandstone (most common for inselbergs) usually weather by shedding large slabs of rock, like fragmented giant plates. If there is no cavity-forming erosion, as in the case of the "Swiss cheese" pockets on limestone, granite and sandstone inselbergs only display continuous forests where the slope is less than 45 degrees, allowing humus to accumulate on the smooth, flat surfaces.

3 - In the Bukhansan National Park north of Seoul, in South Korea, diagonal fault lines allow plants to take root in the spaces where water and humus have accumulated. Several species of shrubs can be found in these faults, including many *Weigela, Lindera, Rhododendron, Callicarpa,* and *Euonymus,* as well as trees such as *Acer, Prunus,* and *Pinus.*

4 - On the granite rocks of Brittany, in France, you frequently find dense populations of *Polypodium cambricum* close to the sea. These ferns spread their branching rhizomes out along the rocky surface. Their erect fronds trap leaves falling from overhanging trees, creating a layer of humus that can be used by the fern's roots. The fronds turn yellow and usually disappear in the summer as the weather turns drier, as is often the case for tropical forest species that undergo a marked dry season. New *Polypodium* fronds appear in early autumn, when the heavy rains start and the dropping temperatures reduce the amount of transpiration. This fern continues to grow through winter and spring.

5 - In Meghalaya in northeast India, ferns dangle their fronds freely from the rock face. Although not directly exposed to the rain, their roots take in the water running over the rock surface.

6 - It's a mistake to think that species growing on vertical rock faces in cold climates can only survive if they anchor their roots deep in the cracks. Just take a look at *Sedum, Saxifraga,* or other *Dianthus* in the higher mountains. They develop on the rock face with only a few roots, mainly for anchorage. Here in the Bukhansan National Park, north of Seoul, this *Davallia mariesii* fern sends its rhizomes crawling out over the rock surface, enduring temperatures below 5°F (−15° C) every winter, with no protection from the snow. On these same vertical rock walls you can find the thick rhizomes of the Saxifragaceae *Mukdenia rossii.*

7 - In the famous Tianmu Shan mountains west of Shanghai one can find rock walls covered by roses, spireas, cotoneasters, rhododendrons, sedums, and even this splendid *Indigofera decora* var. *ichangensis.*

1 - This bellflower, *Campanula rupestris*, grows in the cracks of limestone formations in southern Italy. Most species of bellflower are similarly saxicolous.

2 - On the vast rock formations exposed to high temperatures and full sunlight in the Ceará region of northeastern Brazil, one mainly encounters Cactaceae of the Cereeae tribe, which have anchored into the cracks, as well as a few species of *Tillandsia* whose tufts are affixed directly to the rock surface with short adhering roots. With rain being very rare and erratic, most of the water that these plants receive comes from the nightly dew collecting on the stems, thorns, leaves, and hairs, as well as in the rock's crevices. In the case of *Tillandsia*, the disc-shaped hairs on the leaves capture drops of dew through capillarity, thereby allowing water to be absorbed directly into the leaf.

3 - Most species of *Sedum* grow solely on rock surfaces or in small crevices, such as here in the Luberon in France. Their succulent leaves, thick cuticle, and the stomata that close during the hottest hours of the day allow them to stock up on water and considerably lower their transpiration rate. Many species of *Sedum* and *Sempervivum* tolerate extremely low temperatures and may be installed in vertical gardens in cold, dry climates.

4 - *Everardia montana* is an unusual Cyperaceae that grows solely on the vertical rock walls of *tepuis* in northern South America, as seen here on the cliff at the edge of the Kukenan in Venezuela. I was able to observe the species thanks to the filming of the Ushuaia program with Nicolas Hulot in 1999. In fact, unless you can climb down with ropes as we did, the species lies out of reach. *Everardia* stems hang down 6 feet (2 m) in length, a fourth of that covered in decaying dead leaves. These dry leaves trap minerals and organic particles which in turn are decomposed by microorganisms into nutrients absorbed by the live leaves, stems, and small adventitious roots along the stems.

5 - Gramineae are not only found in vast (horizontal) prairies and savannas. You also come across them on vertical cliffs, such as this species in the Verdon gorges in France. One of the most spectacular is undoubtedly *Arundo formosana*, which only grows on Taiwan's vertical rock walls, hanging down, tightly blanketing the rock. Besides the common *Pogonatherum paniceum* along Asia's waterfalls, other Gramineae, particularly smaller bamboos, are typical of cliffside landscapes.

6 - Silhouettes of *Pinus densiflora* jut out in the late afternoon mists in South Korea's Bukhansan National Park. This species is widely distributed in China, Korea, and Japan, but always in rocky habitats. This is the species that gave rise to woodblock prints and the art of bonsai. Many species of conifers, especially in the genera *Juniperus, Chamaecyparis, Thuya,* and *Pinus*, establish in rocks and on cliffs, both in mountain regions and along the coast. Smaller species and "dwarf" cultivars are perfect candidates for inclusion in a vertical garden, particularly in colder climates, because they can withstand long periods without water in freezing temperatures, thanks to their protected stomata.

7 - Despite what the etymology of their name implies, *Saxifraga* don't break rocks but simply grow on their surfaces and in cracks, as here in the southern Alps. Numerous species colonize the moraines left by receding glaciers.

6

7

1

1 - Even in regions that undergo long dry seasons, associated with savannas and open forests, as in eastern Mali, moist habitats persist in deep fractures, which are reminiscent of the hidden glens of the Mediterranean regions. The flora of Mali's deep crevices shares certain affinities with the humid forests of Guinea, and the presence of several species with short-distance seed dispersal bears witness to the relictual nature of these fragments of humid forest. Along the vertical walls of these moist cliffs, beside the algae and moss – as for instance between these *Ficus* roots – one can find species of *Bolbitis, Lindsaea, Selaginella, Anubias, Begonia, Dissotis, Phyllanthus, Chlorophytum, Oplismenus,* and various Acanthaceae. Climate fluctuations have been quite strong since the Quaternary Era, alternating between long glacial periods (lasting about eighty thousand years) and shorter periods of interglacial warmth (generally only about twenty thousand years). The glacial phases produce colder temperatures in temperate and polar regions and drier conditions in tropical regions, which results in the forests receding in favor of savannas. For more than ten thousand years, we have been in the last warm cycle, called the Holocene epoch. Statistically, we should be reaching the cold cycle soon ... but let's not forget humankind! What will the average temperature be in a couple thousand years after this current phase of global warming, which is most likely connected to our own activities in the world and our dizzying increase in population (keeping in mind that it was as hot, if not hotter, in the Middle Ages)? Perhaps in a few thousand years, if humans are still around and shivering, we will long for the year 2000, when people were so worried about seeing temperatures rise.

2 - It is heresy to cultivate *Cotoneaster, Deutzia, Berberis, Callicarpa,* and *Weigela* species on flat land in deep, rich soil! Anyone who has the opportunity to wander the natural landscapes of China, Japan, and Korea will find that these species grow on slopes, on cliff faces, along waterfalls, or in scree. There barely remain any natural horizontal habitats to be found, after thousands of years of farming. This *Weigela subsessilis* grows on a rockslide near a fast stream in Bukhansan National Park, north of Seoul.

3 - Another *Ficus*: its roots cling to the cliff rocks in the Dogon countryside in Mali. When these species of *Ficus* grow on a cliff or boulder, as here, their roots spread outward and downward, adhering to the rock and absorbing water and mineral salts from within cracks. This opportunistic behavior, common to several species of *Ficus,* probably explains why they are so easy to cultivate. All of these strangler species are good candidates for the upper sections on vertical gardens, especially because their roots can only attach to the irrigation cloth and therefore remain visible.

4 - Immortal? These *Phillyrea latifolia* on the outskirts of Montpellier in France grow on nearly vertical rocky outcrops. New stems successively replace, from the same rootstock, older dying stems (the remnants of which can be seen). Just like the nearby oaks, these trees tend to form a single trunk when they grow on flat land. They will thereby only live a certain amount of time, perhaps several centuries, or even millennia. Their whole conduction system is contained in that single trunk, which thickens as the tree's crown fills out. After a period of time, an imbalance sets in between the mass of foliage situated farther and farther from the roots and the flow of water and mineral salts that need to travel these growing distances. In addition, the weakening associated with the stretching distance makes the trees more susceptible to various pathogens (viruses, fungi, bacteria) and to insects. And so, after only a few centuries (if humans haven't already cut them down), these trees developing on flat ground meet an inevitable death, whereas those growing on vertical rocky substrates tend toward immortality through an indefinite succession of basal shoots. Two important factors preside over their potential immortality. Each trunk has a restricted root system, and the dry season is therefore much more traumatic, so much so that the amount of foliage is kept relatively smaller. Secondly, the angle at which the tree grows allows more light to reach its base, which favors the production of new trunks. As it grows, the new trunk takes over the flow of nutrients because its roots are closer to its foliage compared with the older trees. The older trunks (or stems) stimulate their own replacement by others by gradually sagging, probably increasing the nutritive flow to the latter. No individual dies, merely one of its components. The succession and transmission of traits from one organism to another which it has produced do not necessarily imply death or sexuality.

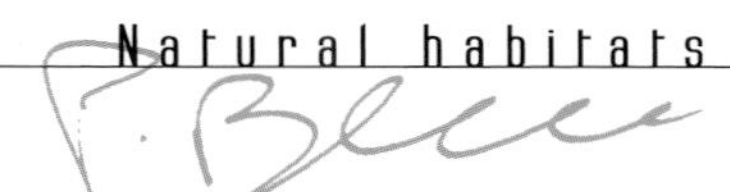

Caves and dark glens

Caves, which are often connected to karst reliefs, result from the differential erosion of the limestone rock. Caves also occur, however, in other geological settings, such as volcanic rocks. But the kinds of habitat found in cave entrances differ from those found on limestone surfaces exposed to wind, light, and repeated droughts. The darkest habitats colonized by plants are cave entrances and deep, narrow gorges. Certain species carpet the bare, humid ground (mostly algae, mosses, and hepatics) while others cling to the steep rocky walls or hang down from overhangs. Rain does not reach these areas; plants establish on seeping surfaces where water percolates through the rock and, on the ground, in areas kept moist by dripping water. Light intensity diminishes away from the cave entrance, and various algae, mosses, hepatics and ferns grow in areas receiving one thousandth the intensity of direct sunlight. Walls in caves that face east or west receive direct light from the rising or setting sun, while those facing north and south receive no direct sunlight. The higher the plants establish on the cave walls, the less light they receive, especially if they hang down from overhangs. The temperature in cave entrances is cooler than the ambient temperature outside, but to what degree depends on which way the cave is facing as well as on the direction of the airflow: it is often between 2 and 5 degrees lower near caves than further out. The air here is usually saturated with humidity, which helps alleviate water stress in the dry season. These are refuge habitats for many moisture-loving species. In Mali, for example, one finds species from the Guinean forests around caves and gorges in the midst of savannas.

Depending on whether they grow on the ground, on vertical walls, or on cave ceilings or overhangs, plant species display different types of architectural patterns. On humid stone walls one finds mostly species that develop an oval-shaped crown of leaves, parallel to the substrate, with the narrow end pointing downward. In certain Gesneriaceae, most notably among Asian *Monophyllaea* and many species of *Streptocarpus* in Africa and Madagascar, each plant grows only a single leaf, maintained above the rock surface by bending out, as in *Streptocarpus*, or by a short stem called a hypocotyl, as in *Monophyllaea*. During the dry season, the single leaf partially dries out and falls back against the rock surface. The tip dries out but the leafblade grows back in the rainy season, starting from the base. The single leaf, which is a cotyledon that grows for the entire life of the plant, is known as a "phyllomorph." Certain species, especially ferns like *Adiantum capillus-veneris*, and *Nephrolepis*, as well many flowering plants such as *Rhipsalis*, *Hoya*, *Columnea*, and *Aeschynanthus* species, grow just as well on oblique or horizontal branches, vertical rock walls, or cave entrance overhangs. These species are generally affixed by their roots to branches or rock crevices, from which they send out their photosynthetic organs, whether cylindrical leafless stems, ribbon-like leaves, or leafy stems. These can be divided into three fundamental categories. In the first, plants merely have chlorophyllus stems either leafless or with small, scale-like leaves. These chlorophyllous stems are cylindrical for many *Rhipsalis* (Cactaceae) and flat in other *Rhipsalis* as well as *Epiphyllum*.

In other cases, the hanging parts are fine stems carrying chlorophyllous leaves. This type of organization, more common among plants, is found in numerous groups. One trait is nonetheless remarkable: the

Ficus natalensis is widespread throughout tropical and southern Africa. Always found in rocky landscapes, it grows erect on exposed cliffs or hangs limp under its own weight along cave ceilings, as here in eastern Mali.

Facing page:
The long green tongues hanging down from stalactites, at the opening to a cave in the Gunung Mulu National Park in Borneo, are *Monophyllaea pendula*. Species in this genus (in the Gesneriaceae family) produce a single leaf that grows indefinitely from its base during the entire life of the plant. Most of the *Monophyllaea* species are strictly confined to limestone cave entrances in Southeast Asia. Most species have a very limited distribution, and most of the species in Gunung Mulu only exist here. This strict endemism translates into an extreme vulnerability to human action.

The entrance of another cave in Gunung Mulu. In the darker areas of the walls, one finds algae, moss, and hepatics as well as a few ferns, *Elatostema* and Gesneriaceae. Beyond the cave, trees from the Dipterocarpaceae family dominate the tall, primary forest.

stems do not grow upward, not even the youngest apex. The top face of the leaf points upward or away from the stem, requiring a twisting of the petiole. This type of organization is exceptional among plants since this is the only case in which the plant turns the underside of its leaves towards the developing apex of the stem.

In addition, certain creepers with adventitious roots hang freely from the branches of host trees or from damp cave ceilings. In Asia, several climbing pepper plants (*Piper*) dangle from cave overhangs, partially closing off the opening. For *Philodendron*, including the common *P. scandens*, the plant only flowers from these hanging stems, as is the case with certain *Scindapsus*, *Rhaphidophora*, and *Monstera* (Araceae). A third organizational mode leads to this type of hanging structure. The stem is contracted through the strong reduction of leaf intervals, and adventitious roots radiate outward to fix the plant to the substrate. From these hang long, narrow, flexible leaves. This type of architecture is primarily found among ferns, with numerous species of: *Asplenium*, *Elaphoglossum*, *Nephrolepis*, *Ophioglossum*, and *Vittaria*, but also among other groups such as *Anthurium*, *Peperomia*, and countless orchids.

Most species found dangling from the rocky overhangs at the cave entrances grow flexible foliage and stems capable of draining the water trickling along their substrate. Their root system is often reduced; its essential role is to keep the plant attached to the surface, since the stems and leaves all contribute to the absorption of water and nutrients. Most of these species can equally be found along oblique branches in moist tropical forests. However, where a drier climate prevents the development of a full epiphytic flora on forest trees, the walls and overhangs of cave entrances are the only habitats available for these pendulous species.

On the vertical rockfaces of the hidden glens of Nice's back country, in southern France, a number of species thrive. Some are merely opportunistic and can be found in various habitats, like many Gramineae and Cyperaceae (with the exception of the famed *Carex grioletii*) and *Geranium robertianum*. Others are more strictly associated with shady, humid biotopes such as the little pimpernel *Anagallis tenella* and several ferns, including *Pteris cretica*, which can only be found in these areas of France.

1 - This photo could really have been taken in any tropical or warm temperate region in the world. The maidenhair fern, *Adiantum capillus-veneris*, grows on wet rocks around caves, waterfalls, or, as here, in the dark glens of the Maritime Alps region of France. It tends to prefer limestone substrates.

2 - On the continually dripping stalactites around cave entrances in Southeast Asia, as here in Gunung Mulu in Borneo, grow numerous species of *Begonia, Homalomena, Rhaphidophora, Globba, Boesenbergia, Pilea, Elatostema, Argostemma,* and *Impatiens,* as well as several Gesneriaceae belonging mostly to the genera *Epithema, Monophyllaea, Chirita,* and *Paraboea.* Several Orchidaceae species of the *Paphiopedilum* genus also grow on the limestone rocks around the caves.

3 - The branching root network of *Ficus natalensis* carpets the ceiling of this cave entrance in Mali. Buds form on these roots, creating new hanging stems. The hanging habit results from the low light intensity, which prevents the stems from thickening. The subspecies *F. natalensis, ssp. leprieurii* displays attractive triangular leaves (it is more commonly known as *Ficus triangularis*) and grows very well on vertical gardens.

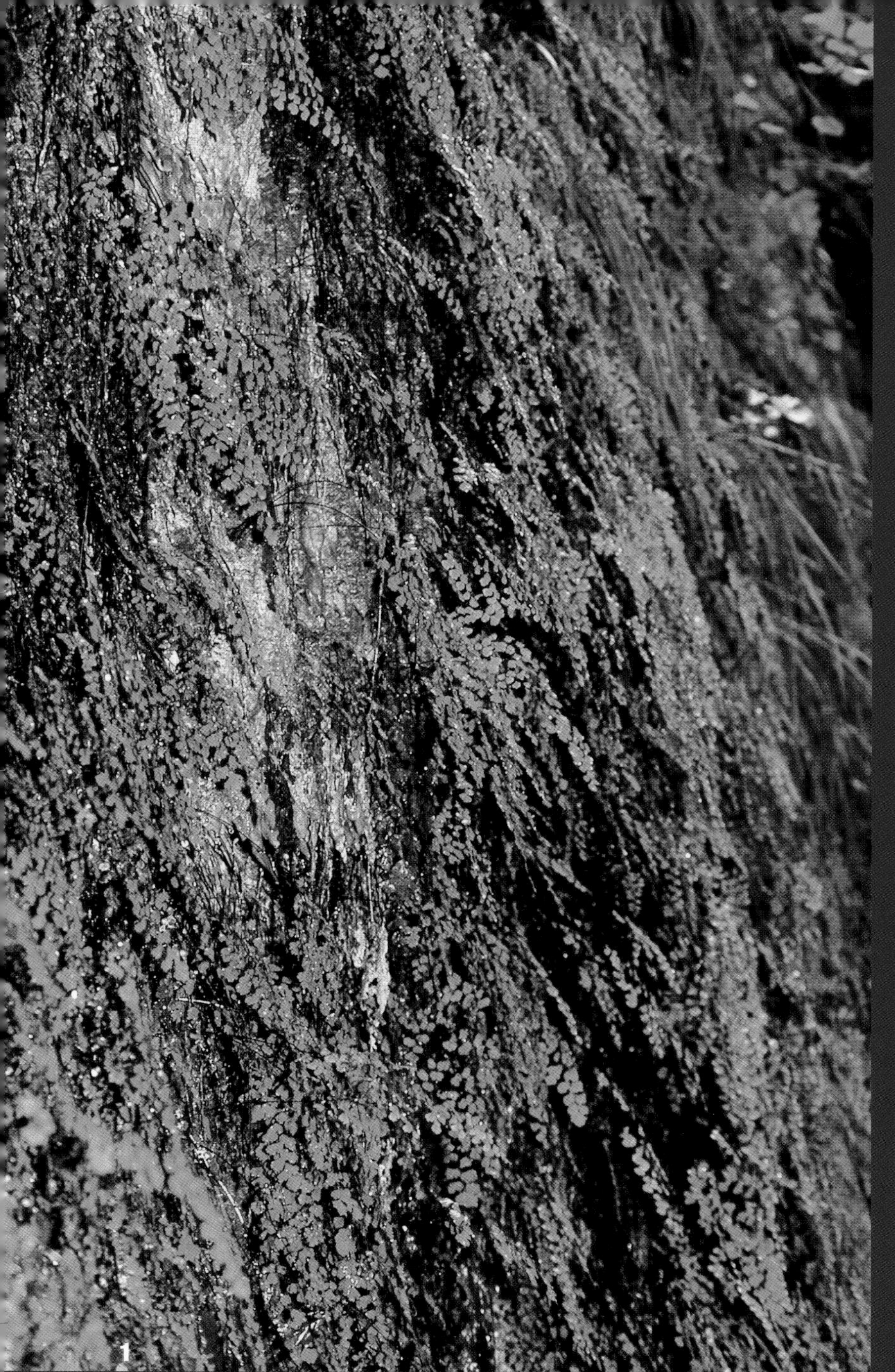

1

2

3

Forest understory

At the scale of herbaceous and shrubby species under 6 feet (2 m) high, the forest understory is a patchwork of different microhabitats. Some of these are free of the leaf litter from the trees above – for example, rocks jutting from the ground, the foot of tree trunks, fallen rotting trunks, the uprooted end of fallen trees, or natural or man-made mounds. But most of the ground surface is covered with leaf litter transforming into a superficial layer of humus.

Lowland forest understories in Europe display a surprisingly low species diversity. Most, in fact, are not even understory plants in the biological sense, since they produce their leaves at the end of winter or beginning of spring, often thanks to the reserves of water and other elements stored in underground tubers. For these species, the leaves receive the direct sunlight that sifts through the leafless branches above. More uncommon are the evergreen species and those that produce leaves in late spring when the canopy is relatively closed off. This is understandable when you consider the annual rainfall in lowland forest areas (or formerly forested areas) such as the Parisian basin: there is about 2 inches (50 mm) of rainfall every month all year round. Two inches is clearly enough for a leafless plant in winter that does not require much water. Yet two inches from June to September is obviously way below the amount required for forest plants to continue growing. During these summer months, understory plants experience a severe shortage of water, and the little water available is quickly being absorbed by nearby tree roots. The few species in Europe's temperate understory that retain their leaves through the summer often have tough, shiny leaves that lower the rate of transpiration, such as holly, ivy, and *Ruscus* (whose leaves are actually flattened stems).

In Europe, it is only in mountain forests, where rainfall is greater in the summertime, that one encounters a wide range of herbaceous and shrubby understory species. This species diversity is similar to, though incomparably poorer than, what is found in the understory of temperate zones with rainy summers, such as in the southeastern United States, the Himalayan foothills, or East Asia (eastern China, Japan, and Korea). Here a rich relictual temperate flora persists, thanks to those humid summers, which are similar to what prevailed at the end of the Tertiary Era in Europe. In temperate zones, the major families of the understory are the Saxifragaceae (in the broader sense), Rosaceae, Ericaceae, Berberidaceae, Violaceae, Liliaceae, Cyperaceae, and most of the fern families.

In tropical regions, understory plant families, with seeds large enough to enable the seedling to push its way through the leaf litter of the forest floor include the following monocotyledons:

Facing page:
Located on the tropic of Cancer, the island of Taiwan is highly mountainous (more than a hundred summits reaching 9,800 to 13,000 feet [3,000 to 4,000 m] high) and extremely humid. It is rare to go two days without a shower. At medium altitudes, vegetation is so dense that it is impossible to enter the understory without stepping on species of *Piper, Elatostema, Pilea, Rubus, Amischotolype, Hemiboea,* or other *Begonia,* not to mention the countless ferns (seven hundred species!). This density, often comparable to that of a vertical garden, is a direct consequence of this high constant rainfall and the lack of dry season. Moreover, the rugged topography allows more direct sunlight to reach the forest floor than in the understory of forests on level ground. This *Begonia aptera* is one of the most common species in the understory northeast of Taipei, among a dozen species of this genus present in Taiwan. Taiwan has a territory that is fifteen times smaller than metropolitan France but has practically the same number of vascular plant species (around 4,500), including more than a thousand (26 percent) that are endemic to the island.

In French Guiana, as in most regions in the humid American tropics, the flat-topped understory boulders are often colonized by a single species, which takes advantage of the humus and water that accumulates on the surface. Beyond species that usually colonize forest floors, such as various species of *Heliconia, Costus,* and *Dieffenbachia,* there are also epiphyte species usually growing on tree trunks, such as this *Philodendron fragrantissimum* at the CNRS research station at the Nouragues camp.

Palms, Araceae, Zingiberaceae, Gramineae, Cyperaceae, Marantaceae, Dracanaceae. As for dicotyledons, these include Rubiaceae, Myrsinaceae, Acanthaceae, Piperaceae, Aristolochiaceae, Euphorbiaceae, and Verbenaceae. As a general rule, monocotyledons display large eye-catching leaves, while dicotyledon shrubs are more discreet. Understory plants are more abundant at the bottom of slopes, where groundwater and air humidity reach higher levels. Other families are confined to unlittered steeply sloped microhabitats since their extremely small seeds, spores, or achenes cannot establish in the presence of leaf litter. However, they easily get stuck in crevices in rocks and bark as well as in the algae, moss, and hepatics growing there. Plants that adopt this reproductive strategy in the understory make up a kind of guild whose principal families include Gesneriaceae, Begoniaceae, Melastomataceae, Urticaceae, Peperomiaceae, several Balsaminaceae, Rubiaceae, Acanthaceae, Bromeliaceae, Araceae, and most fern families. As you can imagine, it is mainly from these families that the species are chosen to be included in vertical gardens, which is itself a vertical structure free of leaf litter.

1 - In the understory of secondary forests, such as here at the edge of an arboretum in Taiwan, this Commelinaceae of South American origin, *Tradescantia (Zebrina) pendula*, often invades embankments, boulders, and tree trunks, sometimes to the detriment of the local flora.

2 - Of the fifty-two species of *Begonia* currently known from peninsular Malaysia, only four can be found outside that territory! This extreme endemism (often reaching 75 to 90 percent of species) is characteristic of many genera, such as *Sonerila, Henckelia,* and *Argostemma.* These are primarily small, saxicolous species with capsular fruits that disperse their minuscule seeds in the immediate vicinity of the mother plant through the action of raindrops. This short-distance dispersal creates isolated populations that tend to become separate species with genetic drift. This *Begonia perakensis*, which grows on shaded boulders along torrents, can only be found in a few spots near Kuala Lumpur.

3 - No, neither a child nor an artist keen on land art haphazardly swabbed these leaves with whiteout! This *Sonerila integrifolia*, like many other understory species, has leaves splashed with white and silvery gray. These stains result from groups of gas-filled epidermal cells that become as refractive as tiny soap bubbles. The adaptive reason for this phenomenon, which is nonetheless frequent in the understory, remains mysterious and may have to do with gas reserves to be used up by the underlying chlorophyllous cells (oxygen accumulated at the end of the day, following photosynthetic activity, and carbon dioxide at the end of the night, resulting from respiration). It may also have something to do with visually repelling plant-eating animals.

4 - In tropical zones with a pronounced dry season, as here in northern Venezuela, plant formations are mostly represented by dense, deciduous forests. In the middle of the dry season, with temperatures going over 95° F (35° C), you might think it was the middle of the winter in temperate forests since none of the trees bear leaves. Most understory plants spend the dry season as tubers underground, but a few species with succulent leaves remain visible, such as this *Sansevieria trifasciata,* which is of African origin but today grows in the rocky understory of many dry forests throughout the tropical world.

In nature, *Hydrangea* species generally grow in the forest understory or along forest edges, mostly on sloping surfaces such as embankments or boulders, as with this species (probably *Hydrangea angustipetala*) colonizing a forest edge in Taiwan at an altitude of 4,900 feet (1,500 m) along with the fern *Gleichenia glauca.*

6

7

8

9

1 - *Selaginella willdenowii* is one of the most common species of Pteridophytes (ferns in the broadest sense) in Southeast Asia's forest understory, as here in Malaysia. It grows on the ground or on slopes, and its metallic-blue iridescence makes it visible from dozens of yards away, among the green and brown leaves blanketing the ground.

2 - A stunning new species of *Begonia* that I discovered in September 2006 on the vertical limestone rocks in the understory in Khao Sok National Park, in southern Thailand. From a distance, I thought it was a fern, its shape reminiscent of *Adiantum* or *Lindsaea*. When I got closer, I saw the texture of the leaves, the nodes in the stems, and its succulence, all indications that this was in no way a fern. I imagined an *Elatostema* or a *Pilea*, because species of these abound in this habitat. But there was no sign of flowering or fruit production and I continued to explore. A few yards farther there was a revelation: at the tips of the branches were tiny white flowers that I could identify immediately, and to my great astonishment, as belonging to a *Begonia*. I collected herbarium samples and took some photos as documentation, which I then sent to Ruth Kiew, the specialist on the *Begonias* of this part of the world. She confirmed not only that it was a new species, but that its biological type, its growth habit, and its general fernlike morphology were unlike any other species of the genus in that area of the world. Luckily the only observed population of this remarkable new species lives in a protected area.

3 - Another *Begonia* species in Khao Sok, *B. integrifolia*, but this one is much more common, and it is one of the few species whose distribution reaches eastern India. Also an understory species, it establishes on slopes or, more often, on limestone rocks, sometimes locking itself for protection in small crevices.

4 - It is easy to understand why the splendid Orchidaceae *Ludisia discolor* grows perfectly in vertical gardens, even when the water is very hard. In nature, it occurs among degraded karstic rocks, in light to very dark forest understory. Such ubiquity is probably related to its vast geographic distribution, covering the Indochina peninsula as well as the Malaysian peninsula. Here it is growing on rocks in peninsular Malaysia.

5 - A young frond of an *Adiantum* in an Andean forest understory, in northern Venezuela. Even if certain species have fully adapted to dry exposed conditions in open habitats or in the forest canopy, the vast majority of ferns grow in the forest understory, on slopes, river banks, boulders, the lower portions of tree trunks, or the forest floor itself.

6 - The liverwort *Conocephalum conicum* grows on wet vertical rocks in Japan's forest understory. Thallous liverworts often create a continuous blanket over rock and shady embankments near waterfalls in both temperate and tropical regions. Nursery staff members do not like to find them growing on their pots, but these plants are one of the most remarkable elements that can be added at the base of a vertical garden.

7 - *Selaginella* species are a typical feature of tropical forest understories. A few species have also diversified in temperate regions, like this *S. denticulata* spreading over a moist slope in France's Maritime Alps.

8 - This *Schizaea elegans* fern grows in the sandy understory soil of the Peruvian Amazon forest. Unlike most ferns, most *Schizaea* species are terrestrial.

9 - The famous *Begonia pavonina* endemic to the Cameron Highlands in the west of the Malaysian peninsula is highly spectacular. It seems to light up the shaded understory because it only reflects the wavelengths for the color blue (about 430 nanometers). It remains difficult to interpret this iridescent phenomenon in terms of adaptation. Blue wavelengths, which are so useful to photosynthesis, only reach the understory in very low intensities and it therefore seems surprising that the plants reflect them. It has been hypothesized that this color repels herbivores, maybe in the same way as reflective metallic paper used in fields and gardens to scare off birds and various insects. Whatever its biological meaning, blue iridescence in the plant world is generally only found in forest understories, in many very different families and in extremely diverse infrastructural modalities, and thus seems to be an adaptive trait.

Forest understory

1 - *Pyrrosia lingua* is a common fern in the warmer temperate regions of Asia, such as southern Japan, China, South Korea, or even here at mid-altitude in Taiwan. It mostly grows on rock surfaces in the forest understory but also establishes on ruins and gently sloping rooftops of forest buildings.

2 - To believe that Bromeliaceae are almost exclusively epiphyte plants disregards a considerable portion of their ecological diversification. Beside ground species belonging to genera such as *Ananas, Bromelia,* and *Puya,* certain genera have well diversified on understory rocks, the most speciose of these being *Pitcairnia,* with over three hundred species. Numerous species of *Pitcairnia* cover near-vertical wet rock faces in the forest understory of the lower Andes and of the Mata Atlantica, like here, close to Rio de Janeiro. They are excellent plants for use in a vertical garden.

3 - Among Zingiberaceae, the saxicolous species belong mostly to the genera *Globba* and *Boesenbergia,* and have considerably diversified in Southeast Asia. In areas with a marked dry season, like the northern monsoon forests on the Indochinese peninsula, plants endure the dry season as tubers clinging to the rock. Where the dry season is less severe, like the southern Malaysian peninsula, Borneo, or Sumatra, species remain sempervirent, or evergreen, generally with smaller tubers. This *Boesenbergia longiflora* grows on wet rocks in the forest understory of northern Thailand. Its roots, mingled with those of other species, cover the rock as they would cover the irrigation cloth of a vertical garden.

4 - *Doryanthes excelsa* is a large Liliaceae in the broad sense that grows in the understory of open forests dominated by different species of *Eucalyptus* on scree and slopes in southeast Australia's Blue Mountains.

5 - *Drynaria bonii* is a fern that clings to rocks in the lighted undestory, often in deciduous forests, as here in Doi Suthep in northern Thailand. The thick rhizome, covered in scales, is protected by sterile papyraceous fronds that dry out without falling off (they are therefore marcescent). These fronds trap dead leaves falling from the canopy and often shelter ant colonies that accumulate plant debris. The fern's roots develop in this dark and moist environment and adhere to the rock. When this shot was taken, it was the middle of the rainy season, and you can distinguish the new, sterile appressed light-green fronds and the base of the erect fertile fronds (which produce the spores), bright green and a little thicker in texture. As with most other species of *Drynaria,* the fertile fronds fall off and disappear at the start of the dry season (in November or December), leaving behind their marcescent median vein, trapping and impaling leaves falling from the canopy above.

6 - *Chirita micromusa* is a small, annual Gesneriaceae that grows on wet rocks in the Indochina peninsula, such as here in the Khoa Yai National Park in Thailand. It germinates at the beginning of the rainy season, usually in June, and then produces a single large leaf. More robust individuals will also produce one or two accompanying small leaves. It flowers in August and fruits in long capsules in September or October before drying out at the beginning of the dry season, at the end of October or beginning of November.

7 - One of the smaller species of unifoliate *Begonia,* meaning it produces a single leaf during its annual cycle. Here we have a population of several hundred individuals, each one originating from a seed, occupying a rock only about two square yards in surface area! This species was observed in Gandhi National Park, north of Mumbai (Bombay), near the Bollywood studios.

8 - Another boulder, another place, another *Begonia.* Yet this *B. sinuata* in Malaysia shows the same development pattern as those in Mumbai, except that its annual cycle is less pronounced since the dry season is much milder in Malaysia.

1

2

3

4

5

6

7

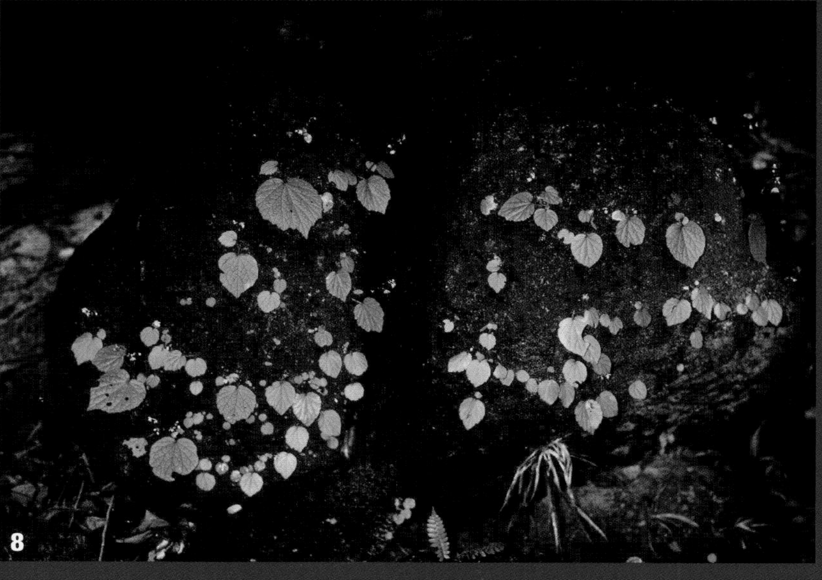

8

1

2

3

Slopes

1 - Without having to travel to the far reaches of the earth, you can find in France, such as here in Normandy, understory banks that are covered in lush vegetation – *Asplenium* (*Phyllitis*) *scolopendrium*, *Polystichum setiferum*, and *Helleborus foetidus* next to small *Ajuga reptans*.

2 - At an altitude of 5,900 feet (1,800 m) in the mountains of northeast Taiwan, the slopes along the trails are covered in various species. Among them, this *Pilea matsudai* is remarkable for its leaf architecture and the broad silvery bands on either side of its median vein.

3 - A detail of the same glen in Normandy, with ferns, ivy, and hellebores covering the slopes. In this rather humid climate, *Asplenium scolopendrium* grows almost to the size of *Asplenium nidus*, its large epiphyte congener of tropical Africa and Asia.

4 - This is not one of my vertical gardens: it's a nearly vertical slope close to a waterfall in Gunung Gedeh, Java. The tall *Curculigo* (or *Molineria*, depending on the authors) *latifolia* blanket the vertical sections along with various *Elatostema* and ferns, while the base is covered with *Colocasia esculenta* and the edges are colonized by *Impatiens platypetala*.

5 - The iridescent green leaves with a purplish central macula on this young *Rubus glomeratus* decorate the slopes along trails in Malaysia's Genting Highlands. In the adult, which climbs into the shrubs of the forest edges, the leaves receive more direct sunlight, eventually losing this coloring.

6 - *Selaginella stipulata* is commonly found on Southeast Asia's humid slopes in areas that are often very dark, as here in Malaysia. The stems, whose growth is determinate and coordinated, bear small overlapping leaves. It ends up resembling a fern with entire leaves or a young palm tree.

7 - In southern Chile, on the slopes of the dense, temperate forests of the great lakes and volcano region (known as the Valdivian forests, after the town of Valdivia), one may see the large fern *Lophosoria quadripinnata*. In Chile, as in other humid, temperate forest blocks of the southern hemisphere (South Africa, southeast Australia, New Zealand), the herbaceous species of the understory are primarily ferns, angiosperms being relatively infrequent. On the other hand, there are a number of shrubby angiosperms. This may be related to the greater vulnerability of the herbaceous species and to their relatively short dispersal distance, thus making it more difficult for them to migrate during climatic fluctuations in order to reach forest refuge areas – themselves becoming smaller and more widely dispersed in these climatic zones. On the contrary, ferns, whose spores are transported on the gentlest of breezes, have been able to take refuge in the smallest patches of relictual forest lands and spread again to new understory areas with the return of the more humid and temperate climate favorable to the development of dense forests.

Epiphytes

The epiphytic life-form is characteristic of tropical forests. In temperate zones, outside of those regions with humid summers such as in eastern Asia, epiphytes are very rare and only represented by a few individuals of species usually found on rocks. The reason generally given for the lack of epiphytes in temperate zones is the severe winter cold. But in fact, saxicolous species growing on rocks often face lower temperatures than epiphytes protected under the forest canopy. It is likely that the dry summers experienced by most of the world's temperate zones are the primary reason for the low epiphyte diversity, since these plants are not so well adapted to drought tolerance as the smaller, compact saxicolous species with their succulent leaves. Nevertheless, there are certain genera of moist temperate forests that include epiphytes, such as *Trochodendron*, *Metrosideros*, *Griselina*, *Astelia*, *Fascicularia*, *Sarmienta*, as well as several species of ferns.

It is thus in tropical forests, particularly in the hyperhumid zones between 3,300 and 6,600 feet (1,000 and 2,000 m), that numerous epiphyte species occur. The very top of the forest is the canopy, the area with the highest concentration of foliage at the periphery of the tree crowns. Whatever its height, a tree that has reached the canopy generally only bears leaves on the outermost 6– to 20-inch-long (15- to 50-cm) branches. On these outer extremities of the tree, epiphytes only include lichens, algae, moss, hepatics, and a few extremely small vascular plants, such as orchids and ferns, since these twigs are not able to support heavier species. There is, however, an immense amount of activity among invisible epiphylls such as the bacteria and fungi covering branches and foliage up in the canopy. They are responsible for the production of many nutrients. As a result, the rainwater that makes it down to the understory is no longer pure. It has become enriched with nitrogen as well as phosphorous, potassium, calcium, and magnesium, to name only the more important elements that plants absorb. Among the organic substances produced one finds carbohydrates, amino acids, and vitamins. Several types of bacteria and blue-green algae (Cyanophyceae) that cover the branches and trunks trap nitrogen from the air and release it as an absorbable substance. According to recent studies, it seems that 30 percent of the nitrogen of the forest's nitrogen cycle is produced by epiphylls in two ways: by its direct fixation by cyanobacteria (blue-green algae) and by the decomposition of all the epiphyll flora. Rainwater trickling down to the leaves, stems, and roots of understory plants is much richer than the rain that falls upon an open prairie. The minerals are absorbed directly into the leaves and branches, through the thin cuticle covering the epidermis, and probably also through the hairs that are often abundant on small herbaceous understory plants.

Underneath the canopy, lies the web of large slanting tree branches. On tall trees in tropical forests, the average height of the bole measures up to 66 or 82 feet (20 or 25 m) and the crown 33 to 49 feet (10 to 15 m). In the latter portion, branches are covered by angiosperms (flowering plants), ferns, moss, hepatics, and lichens, as well as unicellular algae, fungi, and bacteria. It is along these branches, often among the moss, that one can find most well-known epiphytes such as ferns, orchids, and many Bromeliaceae and Araceae. Where the larger branches diverge from the trunk, humus accumulation and mechanical strength allow larger epiphytes to take hold, such as *Philodendron*, *Platycerium*, *Asplenium*, and *Grammatophyllum* species. Apart from the herbaceous species, there are numerous shrubby epiphytes of the Melastomataceae family, with the huge genus *Medinilla* (also speciose in Madagascar), many Ericaceae belonging to the genera *Rhododendron*, *Agapetes*, *Vaccinium*, and *Diplycosia* in Asia, and the genera *Cavendishia*, *Psammisia*, *Sphyrospermum*, and *Satyria* in America. Epiphytic Cactaceae are plentiful, mostly in the genera *Rhipsalis*, *Epiphyllum*, and *Schlumbergera*. They come in the form of long, dangling structures, like many Gesneriaceae, particularly in the genera *Columnea*, *Drymonia*, *Nematanthus*, and *Aeschynanthus*.

It is not an epiphyte species that covers this old oak tree in Normandy but ivy, *Hedera helix*, that attaches its roots all along the trunk. This biological type of vine that creeps up tree trunks with adventitious roots is quite characteristic of the understory of tropical forests, where numerous species of *Piper*, *Marcgravia*, *Freycinetia*, *Philodendron*, *Monstera*, and *Rhaphidophora* make up a vertical and fragmented plant stratum that profoundly marks the tropical forest landscape.

Facing page:
Even in drier climates one can come across a few epiphytes, particularly certain species of Orchidaceae and Bromeliaceae. Here, in western Mali, the limbs of a *Khaya senegalensis* welcome the orchid *Calyptrochilum christyanum*, which is widely distributed throughout most of West Africa's forests. Its long, pearly-white roots collect water from the nighttime dew and the the velamen (veil) that covers them protects them from dehydration during peak daylight hours.

Asplenium nidus is found on trunks and branches, usually a few yards off the ground. Its funnel shape allows humus to accumulate. This funnel created by the foliage of *A. nidus* reaches up to a yard (meter) in diameter. Since we know that between one and two pounds of dead leaves fall yearly on each square yard, this three-square-yard surface may trap and decompose up to six pounds of leaflitter per year. A whole range of smaller epiphytes are associated with the *Asplenium nidus*, creating veritable hanging gardens with each plant in its proper place. These groupings are particularly remarkable in Malaysia. Within the rosette, you often find *Ficus deltoidea*, a small-sized dense shrub growing up to a yard high. *Hedychium longicornutum* spreads out horizontally, along with the long dangling fronds of *Davallia denticulata*. Under the *Asplenium*, in dense shade, hang *Lycopodium phlegmaria*, *Vittaria elongata*, *Ophioglossum pendulum*, and some *Aeschynanthus*. Thus, the whole volume occupied by the *A. nidus* harbors secondary epiphytes drawing water and nutrients from this giant central "sponge."

Hemi-epiphytes also choose to settle in the major forks of trees, starting out as small shrubs and evolving into trees whose crown occupies the center of the host tree crown. These include many species of *Schefflera*, *Clusia*, *Blakea*, *Medinilla*, *Fagraea*, *Ficus*, *Coussapoa*, and *Poikilospermum*. Many species are stranglers, meaning they start out as small shrubs wherever they germinated and then send roots down the trunk. Once they reach the ground, they draw water and mineral salts up to the suspended shrub within the tree's crown. As the hemi-epiphyte shrub continues to grow, its roots multiply and thicken, completely clasping the host trunk, as is the case for many *Ficus* species. More than just preventing the trunk from expanding (the diameter of a tall tree changes only very slowly), the strangler kills as its crown eventually replaces the foliage of the host tree. In fact, the hemi-epiphyte grows outward from a central spot within the tree's crown, eventually covering its host like a giant fungus. The hemi-epiphyte thus impacts its host negatively in three different ways: it shades its foliage, prevents the radial growth of its trunk, and competes with it underground for water and nutrients.

The final stratum as one descends from the canopy to the understory is represented by the herbaceous epiphytes that colonize the first few yards of the trees' trunks. These species are numerous, especially in America where the Bromeliaceae of the understory and median forest zones include various species of the genera *Guzmania*, *Vriesea*, *Aechmea*, and *Neoregelia*. Among Araceae, epiphytic rosulate *Philodendron* species as well as *Anthurium* species (this genus comprising over 800 species) tend to grow in these areas. Also along the trunk base are found various *Peperomia* and a few *Begonia* species as well as countless ferns, notably Hymenophyllaceae and Grammitidaceae.

Facing page:
In the mountains of northeastern Taiwan, at altitudes between 4,900 and 6,600 feet (1,500 and 2,000 m), one finds low forest areas dominated by *Rhododendron formosanum*, with their twisted trunks covered by moss and hepatics. In this fairytale landscape, one also comes across ferns and *Dendropanax* with trilobate leaves.

The image below is, unfortunately, a common sight on the Malaysian peninsula: on vast *Hevea brasiliensis* plantations (of Amazonian origin), only a few indigenous species can establish. On the ground, these are mostly common ferns such as *Nephrolepis biserrata*. The *Hevea* branches, however, are home to a more diverse flora: numerous ferns and orchids, *Hoya*, *Dischidia*, *Ficus*, *Poikilospermum*, and *Medinilla* are among the most representative. *Asplenium nidus* is very frequent in tropical Asian forests, creating a micro-ecosystem as they accumulate humus within the funnel-shaped leaf rosette, trapping leaves as they fall from the trees. Up to many dozens of pounds of humus can accumulate. In this hanging "flower pot" many arthropods, worms, and mollusks flourish, as well as lizards and frogs, while numerous epiphyte plants root in this fortunate spring of humus, thereby creating a population of secondary epiphytes on the *Asplenium*. However, these ecosystems connected with *Asplenium nidus* are always more diverse in primary forest than in *Hevea* plantations.

Following pages:
Left, A branching trunk of a *Rhododendron formosanum* in the mountains of northeast Taiwan. The bark (rhytidome) falls off in strips, taking whole sections of epiphytic moss and hepatics with it.

Right, on a *Chamaecyparis formosensis* trunk, estimated to be about 2,500 years old, a *Trochodendron aralioides* has grown as an epiphyte 50 feet (15m) up, now forming a small rounded tree in the shade of the *Chamaecyparis* crown. *Trochodendron* are often epiphytes on old trees within the primary forests of Taiwan and Japan, but they are also capable of rooting in roadside banks, as is the case for many other epiphyte trees (*Ficus*, *Clusia*, *Schefflera*).

From polar regions to equatorial zones, lichens cover rocks, walls, branches, and trunks. Species vary according to region, but this is the only group of living chlorophyllian organisms (an association of algae and fungus) that has been able to colonize extreme areas to such a degree. These iridescent green lichens are covering shrub branches in Brittany.

1

1 - Even in monsoon forests with a long dry season, epiphytes can be quite abundant, especially in mountainous areas and near streams. These *Platycerium wallichii* are growing on sloping tree branches near the Doi Chiang Dao mountain of northern Thailand. Their erect sterile fronds trap falling leaves from the tree canopy, then close in on them for compacting, rapidly creating humus. The roots of *Platycerium* and other epiphytic ferns penetrate this humus, which provides them with water and nitrogenous nutrients. The hanging fertile fronds are deciduous in the dry season.

2 - *Aeschynanthus longicaulis* (more commonly known as *A. marmoratus*) is an epiphytic species of the Malaysian peninsula, like here in the Khao Sok National Park in southern Thailand. The root system at the base of its stems is often occupied by ants that establish their colony there, although not creating such a complex association as with the South American ant gardens. The ants bring in organic matter that is eventually absorbed by the roots and protect the plant against herbivorous insects as well. As with many other hanging epiphytic species, two types of stems are produced. There are hanging stems as well as stems that travel along the branches with adventitious roots. These affixed stems then produce new hanging stems. This *Aeschynanthus longicaulis* is one of the best epiphyte species for shady areas on a vertical garden. I find it difficult imagining a tropical vertical garden without it.

3 - *Psychotria serpens* is found throughout the warm temperate Far East: in southern Japan, in southeastern China, and here in Taiwan. This is one of the rare temperate species of this immense tropical genus (more than a thousand species). *Psychotria* display a variety of life-forms, but the vast majority of species are understory shrubs in humid tropical forests. This *P. serpens* belongs to a small group of understory climbing species that cling like ivy or *Philodendron*, attaching themselves with small, adventitious roots. Yet they sometimes act more like an epiphyte or saxicolous plant, at least in their early stages.

4 - At an altitude of nearly 8,200 feet (2,500 m), at Doi Inthanon in northern Thailand, you can find a spectacular shrubby epiphytic Rubiaceae in bloom during monsoon season, this one in August of 2006. As with *Mussaenda*, the attractive flowering parts colored white on this *Hymenopogon parasiticus* are not petals but extensions of a sepal. Despite the species' name, the plant is not a parasite but an epiphyte, causing no harm to its tree host.

5 - With more and more uses for palm oil these days, tropical forests are receding in the face of extending oil palm plantations (*Elaeis guineensis*, of West African origin). Flying over the Malaysian peninsula, what seems like forests are usually low-altitude plantations of *Hevea* and *Elaeis*. Along roads, you can drive for hundreds of miles and only see these plantations. At least there is more animal and plant diversity in these tree plantations than in corn or manioc fields, but it is still much lower than what is found in forests, even secondary forests. The aspect is deceptive, since along the trunks (stipes) of palm trees, numerous epiphytes grow in the axils of broken, dead leaves. But these epiphyte species are primarily common ferns belonging mostly to the *Nephrolepis, Polypodium, Davallia,* and *Pyrrosia* genera. And yet it was this spectacle, commonly seen in Malaysia, that captivated me thirty-five years ago, in the summer of 1972. And this palm stipe covered in epiphyte ferns reminds me in some odd way of my plant columns.

Epiphytes

1 - Epiphytes are amazingly numerous in eastern Madagascar's dense, humid forests, such as here at the well-known Andasibe station. With the forest being low (the canopy is often no more than 50 feet [15 m] high), epiphytes can easily be observed a few yards up. Apart from orchids, it is the genus *Medinilla* that, with at least seventy endemic species, characterizes this epiphyte symusia. Ferns and associated groups, such as Lycophytes, are also quite well represented here and this *Lycopodium* (or *Huperzia* for some specialists) develops stems lined with small foliar structures, each stem at first growing upwards before stooping downward under its own weight.

2 - This *Rhipsalis* of the *R. cassutha* group is an epiphytic cactus! It may be surprising to learn that within the family of Cactaceae, several genera consist of epiphytes, and many species grow only in the humid tropical forests of Central America, the Amazon, and the Mata Atlantica in southeast Brazil. It is in the Mata Atlantica, in the outskirts of Rio de Janeiro, that the genus *Rhipsalis* is the most diversified. It is difficult to go a few yards in the forest without coming across three or four different species. These hanging plants drain water as it trickles from the canopy. Their cylindrical or flattened stems are often covered by green algae because they are constantly wet. The various species of *Rhipsalis* thrive in vertical gardens.

3 - An orchid, probably of the *Vanda* genus, growing on a tree trunk in northern Thailand, sends out roots that cling tightly to the trunk. Orchids display numerous adaptations for epiphyte life, such as succulent water-storing leaves covered by a thick cuticle that lowers transpiration, pseudo-bulbs that store water as well as minerals and organic substances (absent in *Vanda*), or thick chlorophyllian roots covered by several layers of epidermic cells. These reflect infrared light, preventing overheating. This silvery-white veil is also able to absorb the nightly dew, the only source of water during the dry season.

4 - In Gabon, this *Rhektophyllum* (which is now placed in the *Cercestis* genus) *camerunense* is a creeper of the Araceae family, growing on trunks in the understory, just like *Philodendron* and *Monstera* in America or *Rhaphidophora* and *Scindapsus* in Asia. The slender base of the stem ends up dying off and the only ground contact comes from the long feeding roots hanging vertically down along the trunk. Plants behaving this way (germination on the ground, climbing growth, followed by necrosis of the stem base) are often called "secondary epiphytes" to differentiate them from those species that germinate directly on the trunk or on branches.

5 - Unlike most other species of *Hoya,* which are epiphytic creepers, *Hoya linearis* hangs freely from branches in mid-altitude mountain forests of the eastern Himalayas. Like many *Columnea* and *Aeschynanthus,* they produce lateral stems that crawl out along the relatively horizontal branches. From these rooted stems they send down other hanging stems.

6 - In Sumatra these *Platycerium coronarium* have grown in the forking branches of a tall tree, which is starting to perish slowly due to the surrounding deforestation. This species of *Platycerium* is one of the most efficient in its genus at creating its own suspended humus, thanks to its vast sterile fronds reaching up like hands toward the sky. When they dry out, the fronds retract downwards, picking up dead leaves and other fallen debris along the way.

7 - In the forests surrounding the Ngorongoro crater in Tanzania, the nightly dew condensation allows for lichens from the *Usnea* group to proliferate, hanging freely from the branches like *Tillandsia usneoides* (perfectly named) in America. This convergence of lichen and angiosperm is quite remarkable.

8 - Nearly horizontal branches create perfect support structures for a large number of epiphytes, especially ferns such as these *Pyrrosia* and *Drynaria* mixed with *Hoya,* on the island of Koh Samui in southern Thailand.

8

1

2

3

4

5

6

7

1 - *Philodendron lacerum,* native to the Greater Antilles, has become naturalized in Penang botanical garden, Malaysia. It is not in fact an epiphyte species in the strictest sense, but a creeper climbing vertically up the tree trunks and attaching to the bark (rhytidome) with adventitious roots appearing at the nodes. Quite often, the lower 6 feet (2 m) of the main stem dies, resembling epiphyte behavior. But a quick examination reveals that these stems have feeding roots in contact with the ground, most of them issuing 6 to 9 feet (2 to 3 m) above the ground. As you can see in this view, other long nutritive roots reach the ground from 40 feet (12 m) high. This species thus progressively becomes a secondary epiphyte.

2 - *Philodendron insigne* is a very common species in the forests of French Guiana. It is an epiphytic *Philodendron* species in the strictest sense. Unlike *Anthurium,* which are almost exclusively epiphytes, the vast majority of the five hundred *Philodendron* species are creepers that climb using adventitious roots. *P. insigne* is remarkable in its growth pattern. It forms a vertical succession of leaf rosettes 3 to 6 feet (1 to 2 m) apart, each one resembling a unique and independent epiphyte. Examining the entire plant, you find that each upper rosette is growing from a fine stem with reduced leaves emitted from the rosette below it. This axis grows vertically, clinging to the trunk by its roots, before increasing its leaf size and forming a new rosette above it.

3 - Orchids are the best-known family of epiphytic plants, as well as the most diverse. Species can be found in all types of tropical forest habitats, but it is primarily in the humid tropical forest at mid-altitude (between 2,600 and 5,000 feet [800 and 1,500 m]) that the number of species explodes. This is mainly due to the higher rainfall and the frequency of nighttime mist. This *Dendrobium* with articulated pseudo-bulbs covers the tree branches in the low forest of Doi Inthanon's summit, at an altitude of more than 8,200 feet (2,500 m), in northern Thailand.

4 - The epiphyte world of America's tropical forests is characterized by Bromeliaceae. Less numerous in the Amazon lowland forest than in forests of the Andean foothills, the mountains of Central America, or the Mata Atlantica, they are nevertheless quite diversified in all types of forests, with the exception of dry forests. In French Guiana, at the Nouragues research site, this *Streptocalyx longifolius* is one of the species frequently encountered in suspended "ant gardens," benefiting from the reciprocal relationship between plant and ant.

5 - In the Canary Islands, the different species of *Aeonium* colonize mostly rocky habitats, slopes, cliffs, and even roofs, but some grow as epiphytes, such as these *Aeonium subplanum,* which germinated in the axils of old broken leaves of a *Phoenix canariensis,* the Canaries' famous date tree, on the island of La Gomera.

6 - Just like *Rhipsalis, Epiphyllum* is an epiphytic cactus genus of the forests of Central and South America. *Epiphyllum phyllanthus,* often associated with ant gardens, is widespread throughout the Amazon and surrounding regions, such as here in the *Mata Atlantica* near Rio de Janeiro.

7 - *Polypodium subauriculatum* is a common epiphytic fern in Southeast Asia, as here near the Khao Sok National Park in Thailand. This species is reminiscent of various *Nephrolepis,* but its dangling fronds are generally wider and longer. Often growing as a secondary epiphyte at the base of a *Drynaria* or *Platycerium,* it is an eye-catching element of Asia's epiphyte flora. Rarely stocked by horticulturists, it is, however, an excellent species for a vertical garden.

2

The impact of plants on architecture

The various "strangler" species of *Ficus* germinate in the crown of the host tree, often in forking branches, and gradually wrap their roots around the trunk, as here on the island of Koh Samui in Thailand. Since they are not parasites and do not feed directly at the expense of the host tree, several species of strangler *Ficus* may indifferently establish on trees, rocks, or buildings. The tensions created by the roots eventually loosen the stones in the wall.

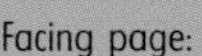

Facing page:
Even though their proportions and enveloping character are spectacular, these *Platycerium wallichii* have only a slight destructive impact on the ceramic dragons jutting out from the Doi Chiang Dao caves in northern Thailand. Their thin roots grow solely in the humus that accumulates in the sterile fronds.

From superficial impact to overall destruction

Several studies have shown that the ancient walls of older dwellings and buildings such as churches, as well as retaining walls for various structures such as those supporting railroad tracks, were likely to host a flora comparable to what is found on natural cliffs and rock slides. This saxicolous flora often has a destructive impact on the structures, especially in tropical regions. In temperate zones, the colonizing species are mostly herbs and small shrubs, such as various Gramineae, Crassulaceae, bell flowers, carnations, wallflowers, and corydalis. Apart from a few species brought in from the Far East or garden escapes, such as certain species of *Cotoneaster* and *Pyracantha,* and above all the well-known *Buddleja davidii,* which has become invasive in various regions of Europe since the 1930s, few woody species colonize these old walls. This probably has something to do with the fact that shrubby and arborescent species on cliffs and in rocky zones are scarce in Western Europe, unlike in the Far East, because of Europe's drier summers. The fossil records show that toward the end of the Tertiary Era, between only five and ten million years ago, Western Europe's climate was warmer and more humid than it is today. The temperate forests harbored a rich flora at that time, whereas today these plants are only found in relictual form in the southeastern United States, in the Himalayan foothills, and in the Far East in a zone stretching from South Korea through southern Japan to eastern China, around Shanghai. Most of our garden plants come from those areas, but extra watering is required in the summer in order to recreate the climatic conditions of their native habitats. Out in nature, many of these exotic species are confined to exposed rocky habitats. Only a few of them are adapted to drier conditions – the glossy leaves of the *Cotoneaster,* for example – enough to establish up walls on buildings. *Buddleja* presents a different case, since it usually grows in damper zones such as around gutters or in seeping cracks, where its roots may cause severe damage.

Apart from a few herbaceous plants such as bellflowers or various *Cerastium, Aubrieta, Bergenia, Iris, Sedum,* and *Sempervivum,* very few species are deliberately planted on walls, generally on low walls surrounding yards, never on the exterior walls of homes. The only species deliberately planted to cover walls are creepers planted along the base that then grow up the wall with the help of short, adventitious roots (ivy, bignones, climbing hydrangeas) or with tendrils secreting an adhesive substance, as is the case with Virginia creepers (*Ampelopsis* and *Parthenocissus*). Sometimes, too, wisteria and honeysuckle are planted at the foot of gutters and wrap their stems upward, working their way around other support structures along the way, such as metal balcony frames. The root systems of these creepers grow underground, but their shoots enter between stones and under roof tiles, sometimes prising them apart, which is why creepers are generally pruned so that they do not cover more than just the wall. Once they have wrapped themselves around a support structure, the twining species exert a mechanical strain, deforming the structure over time or even breaking it apart. Yet their dense foliage protects the wall from heavy storms.

In tropical cities many lush herbaceous and shrubby species are planted into sidewalk containers, as in the old districts of Bangkok and other Asian cities. Between the central lanes allocated to the traffic and the sidewalks, one can find an uninterrupted line of plants in containers

Algae and moss quietly colonize the humid concrete walls where rain waters seep from a pipe in Hong Kong.

The venerated *Ficus religiosa,* of Indian origin, is one of the most common species of strangler *Ficus* in tropical Asia, since it grows both on mineral substrates (both natural and artificial) and on trees, in equatorial climates as well as in tropical monsoon climates. This famous head of Buddha gently wrapped in *F. religiosa* roots in Wat Mahathat is the symbol of Ayutthaya's glorious past as the former capital of the kingdom of Siam.

two to three feet wide. These continuous lines of plant containers, reaching 6 to 9 feet (2 to 3 m) high at times, act as a living screen, offering a surprising sense of well-being and conviviality against the noise and pollution created by vehicles. Very few creepers are planted, however, in tropical cities, understandably, since they would develop too quickly in such humid environments and damage the fragile facades already blighted by the torrential rains. Apart from the algae, mosses, and ferns that cover damp walls without causing deterioration, some woody species establish on the buildings and damage them. These are mostly various species of *Ficus*, which were originally hemi-epiphytic species growing in tree crowns. It is mostly Southeast Asian cities that are thus being invaded by two species of *Ficus*, *F. religiosa* (the sacred *Ficus* of pagodas) and *F. benghalensis*, both of which are native to India. Those species are naturally very abundant in the dense, deciduous forests on the dry mountain slopes of the Western Ghats.

It seems that humans are continually confronted with this duality: how to surround ourselves with plants without letting them propagate freely. And yet it is precisely this form of freedom of the plant world that most fascinates us.

Without changing its structure, algae and moss cover a sculpted stone statue in Kanazawa cemetery in Japan.

Superficial impact

1 - Along the joints between roof tiles, moss grows in the form of small cones standing an inch high, in the extremely humid atmosphere of the Welsh countryside in Great Britain.

2 - Algae and moss grow along the cement joints in a stone wall in Crato, in northeastern Brazil. Quite often, the roughness of the cement favors spore germination and the adherence of algae and moss rhizoids (special hairs that both secure and feed the plant like tiny roots). Only older concretes that have had their alkaline content washed away by rain are likely to harbor plant life.

3 - Here is another splendid *Adiantum capillus-veneris*, which tolerates urban pollution and seems as much at home on an old concrete wall seeping water on a Hong Kong apartment building as it does on wet limestone rocks in the Maritime Alps region of France or near waterfalls in most tropical countries.

4 - In the Bronx Botanical Garden in New York City, algae and moss grow between the hexagonal concrete paving stones.

5 - The rugged countryside and frequent earthquakes in Japan have triggered the construction of innumerable structures to protect trafficked roads. Roadsides are frequently stabilized by concrete curtains fortified by a square mesh, such as here on Kyushu Island. This heterogeneous support invites the spontaneous installation of various algae and moss species.

6 - Without going all the way to Monaco, where this photograph was taken, you can find the small saxicolous fern *Asplenium trichomanes* on shaded rocks and old stone walls in most European regions. With its weak root system, it is a well-mannered guest that never becomes destructive.

7 - Artificial lighting set up by humans always affects plant behavior. In temperate zones, trees situated near public lamps remain green longer in the autumn, while shaded walls that are artificially lit welcome a halo of algae and moss. In caves throughout the world, such as here in Borneo, fluorescent and incandescent lights help plants develop – mostly algae, moss, hepatics, and ferns, whose spores enter the caves on the gentlest breeze.

8 - At the height of Normandy's winter, with its raised humidity levels and ambient coolness, Trouville's roofs cover over in green algae. They dry out in the summer, but the fine layer of humus filling the micro-interstices creates a favorable substrate for the establishment and proliferation of algae in autumn.

9 - The monsoon regions of Asia, and most particularly on the Indochinese peninsula, are the areas where Zingiberaceae of the *Curcuma* and *Kaempferia* genera are the most diversified. While the *Curcuma* grow primarily on the ground, *Kaempferia* are often saxicolous, and their small rhizomes work their way into the cracks in the rock. At the Beng Melea temple, in the Angkor region, these *Kaempferia* are only found on walls where they grow between the stones without loosening them. Since these plants are never found on nearby level ground, these ruins are in some way a protective refuge for the species.

10 - In the Yerabatan Palace, an underground water reservoir in Istanbul, some of the tall underwater columns are sculpted. In order to highlight these sculpted areas, an incandescent light is placed close by, entailing the development of superficial and innocuous green algae.

1

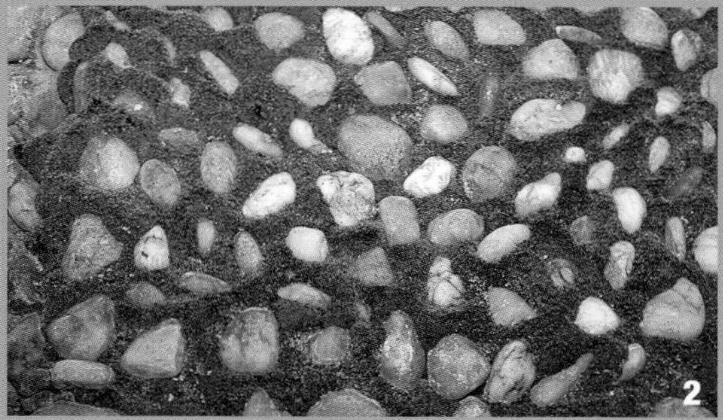

2

3

4

5

6

7

8

9

10

7

Hazardous impact

1 - Along building gutters are the best places for plants to establish on walls, since the successive joints are not always completely sealed. The leaks increase as rain pours down daily during monsoon season, as here in Mumbai. Mumbai receives an average of 27 inches (69 cm) of water in July, which is more than Paris gets in a year. Among the plants to be found here, there are those with no destructive impact, such as ferns (mostly *Pteris vittata*), and others that will eventually loosen the stones and penetrate the gutter, such as *Ficus benghalensis*. The *Ficus* must be cut way back each year to maintain building walls, restrain their root development, and prevent heavy weight on any one area of the façade.

2 - On Biarritz's old stone walls facing the sea, various halophile plants thrive, either enjoying or tolerating the sea spray that regularly deposits salt on their leaves and roots. Among them, the most common are *Crambe maritima* and *Senecio cineraria*, the silver ragwort, of Mediterranean origin.

3 - On old village walls in France, the bellflower *Campanula portenschlagiana* of Balkan origin reseeds itself and grows between the stones. The creeping stems become long stolons that wind their way between the stones and through the wall. Yet they don't cause any damage because the roots and stem bases barely grow in diameter.

4 - During the rainy season, the Angkor temples come to life. The gigantic *Tetrameles* sprout foliage, like *Lagerstroemia* and various tuberous herbaceous species, while algae, moss, hepatics, and ferns cover the stones. Among the most common species at forest temples such as Beng Melea, *Elatostema* covers most of the lower walls, producing long succulent leafy annual stems, like in *Begonia* or *Impatiens*. It spends the dry season reduced to its flat circular tuber, pinned to the stones.

5 - Native to Mexico and Central America, *Tradescantia* (more commonly known as *Rhoeo*) *spathacea* became naturalized in many Asian regions and frequently colonizes old walls and ruins, such as here in Ayutthaya in Thailand. It is efficiently dispersed by ants that carry the seeds into favorable micro-sites, within close range of the mother plant. The more light there is the more their leaves stand erect to shade from the light and reduce transpiration. Their succulent leaves survive the dry season. Considering this is a herbaceous monocotelydon (and thus incapable of increasing the diameter of its stem), the species has very little destructive impact on buildings.

6 - The caper tree, *Capparis spinosa*, is one of the few temperate species of this immense tropical genus. It grows only on vertical structures in Mediterranean regions and its natural habitat is mainly seaside cliffs. But this species can also be found in towns, such as here in Lecce, in southern Italy, where it ends up creating broad tufts of stems hanging down 6 feet (2 m) on the walls. The stems themselves only live a few years, but new ones constantly develop from the woody stock anchored in the wall. The roots penetrate deeply between the stones, but their destructive impact remains low because the stock rarely grows more than 4 inches (10 cm) in diameter. The stems and roots also create a long-term stabilizing force for the wall.

7 - The roof tiles and gutters of the villages of northern Tenerife, in the Canary Islands, are home to large populations of *Aeonium ciliatum*. These Crassulaceae have a weak root system and their destructive impact remains quite low, compared with their relatively imposing dimensions.

1

2

3

4

Destructive impact

1 - In Colaba, Mumbai's historic district, old colonial buildings often bear the destructive impact of two species of *Ficus*, *F. benghalensis* and *F. religiosa*. On this façade you see a young *F. religiosa* whose roots have worked their way between the stones and the signboard. If the enveloping roots of this strangler *Ficus* latch on and stabilize the stonework, those that penetrate between the stones tend to displace them as they thicken. Everything happens as though the wall were transforming into a living being through internal growth within an exoskeleton.

2 - On a former rum distillery near Cayenne in French Guiana, *Philodendron acutatum* covers the brick walls as it branches out. Though they do not thicken, many roots propagate into the brickwork, lending a new fluidity to the increasingly weakened wall.

3 - Who would have imagined that this small plant is in fact the younger stage of a mighty *Ficus benghalensis* that recently established inside the crack of a wall in Mumbai? Needless to say, further root development will expand the crack.

4 - The famous *Tetrameles nudiflora* that grow on the Angkor temples usually germinate on large boulders in nature, especially in tropical Asia's monsoon forests. The Angkor temples, many abandoned for more than seven hundred years, were built with sandstone from the mountains near Phnom Kulen (today protected as a national park). *Tetrameles* thus find the same conditions in these ruins as in Phnom Kulen. The *Tetrameles* roots wrap around the walls and stabilize them. Walls crumble mostly when the trees are cut away to clear off the temple. In fact, walls that were once protected by the stable conditions of the forest understory suffer from the sharp fluctuations in temperature and humidity once exposed to light and heavy rain. Dead roots from cut-down trees retract as they dry out between the stones, leaving open spaces and causing greater instability. Clearly deforestation in these temple sites must be immediately accompanied by restoration, or the walls will gradually crumble. That is what is happening today at this Beng Melea temple, which was partially deforested during the filming of the movie *Two Brothers*, without any subsequent restoration.

5 - Besides *Tetrameles*, *Lagerstroemia calyculata* are among the most frequent trees in Angkor's ruins. The destructive impact of the *Lagerstroemia*, though somewhat less visible, is in fact more pronounced than the impact of *Tetrameles* for two main reasons. On the one hand, *Lagerstroemia* are not very stable and often fall onto walls, destroying them and padding the rocks with woody extrusions where they continue growing. Furthermore, their roots deeply penetrate the structure, displacing the stones as they grow in diameter, unlike the *Tetrameles* whose roots weave around the stones before branching out and stabilizing in the ground.

6 - In an island cave in Along Bay, which once served as a hospital during the Vietnam War, run-down gutters are often overrun with *Ficus* roots seeking water and nutrients. As the roots grow in diameter, they break apart the gutters..

Destructive impact

1 - This particular individual of *Tetrameles nudiflora* is one of the stars at the Ta Phrom temple in Angkor. Its enormous, enveloping roots seem terribly destructive, while in fact they wrap around entire sections of wall without exerting any squeezing force, which would cause compression and crumbling. Unlike many other trees, the radial growth of the roots happens on the surface and not inside the substrate, which is why the ruins are stabilized. Cutting down the trees without immediately restoring the site would be the ruin of these temples.

2 - This *Ficus religiosa* in Mombai wrapped its roots around the trunk of its host tree, then the railings, then the small wall along the sidewalk, and finally covered part of the sidewalk. In many tropical cities such unexpected tree growth draws neither indignation nor anger resulting in the removal of the individual plant. Quite the contrary, they are woven into the urban fabric and you frequently find walls restored around a tree trunk or roots. Similarly, walls are often painted, covering roots and climbing stems. This cohabitation of human-built edifices and free, uninvited nature is only seen with plants a few inches tall in our western societies. We only accept herbaceous species such as bellflowers, cineraria, or corydalis on our walls. In the tropics, plants take over a yard or tens of yards as trunks and roots that are solid as concrete. Curiouisly, only a few climbing plants are deemed attractive to our eyes.

3 - A strangler *Ficus* (probably *F. gibbosa*) has ended up killing its *Tetrameles* host in the Ta Phrom temple in Angkor. On this same site, three events thus took place in succession: the construction of a wall, the germination and growth of a first tree, and finally, today, the flourishing of a second tree, all in a space of less than a thousand years. These *Ficus* begin their development as creepers attached to the stones with their adventitiouis roots. They are a particular menace to monuments because their stems branch out and work their way into the smallest cracks. This *Ficus* species is able to produce several trunks at a distance, all from the same germinated seed. As the roots become thicker, they prise open the stones of the wall. This *Ficus* is probably one of the most destructive species for the Angkor monuments.

1

2

3

3

The vertical garden

From the idea to the concept

Regardless of the Bible translation, verses 17 to 19 in the third chapter of Genesis are hardly joyful! In a nutshell, after being expelled from Eden, poor Adam and his descendants must cultivate the earth with sweat on their brows, fighting brambles and other weeds, in order to grow and harvest seeds in the field. And yet, everything had been so simple and carefree before that original sin: a river flowed through Eden and countless trees grew that were "pleasant to the eye and good to eat." This Eden must in fact have resembled agro-forests, those cultivated forest systems that still persist in certain tropical regions, assembling a variety of useful species. Their upkeep requires a great knowledge of plants but a minimal work investment. Ultimately, that bite out of the apple somehow forced us to pass from a system of picking food to an economy of more intensive cultivation. Humans, in their cleverness, have of course succeeded in producing an increasing amount of food from the earth, all the while working less and less and with little regard to depleting resources. We are forgetting the duties handed down to us in connection with original sin. However, even today what gardener would not be proud recounting in minute detail the work required in order to obtain such beautiful plants? In the collective imagination plants are understood as the fruit of man's labor, whether vegetable, flower, fruit, tuber, grain, or timber. Haven't we often heard the claim made by forest rangers that forests left untended (by humans, obviously!) risk not regenerating harmoniously and dying out? Oh, the vanity! We forget that people have only been tending to the woods for a few centuries, whereas the forests themselves have existed since the Devonian Period, during the Paleozoic Era, in other words for more than 350 million years.

Today, more than half of the human population on earth lives in cities. All references to nature or to agricultural systems tend toward increasing obscurity. Images of agriculture are only present in the minds of those who live in certain villages that are remote or carved into rugged topographies. The mechanization of agriculture, once the privilege of Western societies alone, is now being undertaken in numerous, so-called emerging countries. Today, a resident of Bangkok or Saõ Paulo knows as little about agriculture as a resident of Paris or New York. Thus, that old Judeo-Christian notion narrowly binding earthly soil to an agricultural productivity prized by humans, an element in fact in most other belief systems, has started to disappear due to a lack of direct models. On the other hand, the untamed wilderness remains an active image, routinely and positively depicted in magazines and countless television documentaries. These are the images of "before. . . ."

Today, in fact, humans are still arrogant, certain that they are responsible for all of Earth's troubles. Humans are so powerful, so intelligent, etc., etc. . . . Our status approaches that of gods in our ability to disrupt climates. Why not compare ourselves to Zeus, Poseidon, or Aeolus? The climate is warming up and we know that it is hot in hell. Humans have brought about Evil; can we figure out how to bring about Good as a form of redemption in order to return to the tranquility of the past? Will the Earth forgive us? But why do we ignore the fact that in the Middle Ages, the temperatures were slightly higher than today's averages? Or that five thousand years ago it was about 4° F (2° C) warmer? Certainly, if we refer back to the "little ice age" that occurred approximately between 1650 and 1850, the average temperatures have risen, but only by about 1° F (0.7 to 0.8° C) since the end of that period, corresponding to the start of the industrial age.

The concentration of carbon dioxide is rising, as we all know: from 280 parts per million (ppm), it has reached nearly 380 ppm in a century and a half. Cabbages planted today grow about 25 percent faster than those that were planted by our great-grandparents! In fact, so long as there is light, water, and mineral nutrients, plant growth is directly proportional to the rate of carbon dioxide present, at least until the level of concentration reaches 800 ppm. That is why farmers spend so much money adding carbon dioxide to greenhouses. However, this rise in carbon dioxide concentration also has hidden side effects, like stimulating the growth of already fast-growing plant species. These pioneer species, invasive at times, are capable of establishing and developing rapidly in places that have been recently disturbed. The burst of growth that follows and the ensuing fierce competition tend to eliminate the slower-growing species, with a negative impact on biodiversity. As regards the effects on the tall forest trees of the canopy, it can be feared that the increasingly high concentration of carbon dioxide, causing an extra development of the foliage during the growth phase (in spring in temperate regions and in the rainy season in tropical regions), will eventually produce an imbalance of the sap flows. The risk is then that the crown of the taller trees will become more vulnerable to strong winds, and the trees themselves more likely to fall as a result. The global increase in carbon dioxide, as we know from expert reports, is the result of human activity, primarily in industrialized nations. We must keep in mind, though, that every human being, whether rich or poor, breathes out the same amount of carbon dioxide. So, per square kilometer, India releases twelve times more carbon dioxide from human metabolism than the United States (about 1.2 billion people on 3.3 million km^2 in India and about 300 million people on about 10 million km^2 in the US).

As for ocean levels, with an increase of 4 to 8 inches (10 to 20 cm) over the last century, are we really so far from average fluctuations measuring approximately 328 feet (100 m) every 100,000 years (the average duration of glacial-interglacial periods)? That is precisely 4 inches (10 cm) per century. Where would today's coastal populations be if ocean levels reached 20 feet (6 m) higher, as was the case only 125,000 years ago? Yet during the last glacial maximum, around 15,000 to 20,000 years ago, the ocean levels only reached the continental plateau, about 400 feet (120 m) below current levels. If that facilitated human migration, plants and animals also profited from the available routes for migration: between Malaysia, Sumatra, and Borneo, for example, my cherished *Cryptocoryne* were able to colonize new riverbeds and diversify into new species through genetic drift.

But independently of such aspects of climatic evolution and humanity's role in such an evolution, we are undoubtedly responsible for modifications in the landscape the world over, excepting certain deserts, high mountains, and tundra regions that have been of little interest to us. Each modification entails the destruction of local vegetation, affecting a range of animals and microorganisms, in favor of various forms of agricultural exploitation. Certainly, we have not yet achieved the pessimistic forecasts from the 1980s, which predicted a near-total disappearance of tropical forests by the year 2000. And yet the deterioration is spectacular! Certain environments, such as floodplain forests, karst forests, and flat lowland forests, are shrinking rapidly. As we know, most countries choose to protect lands that are difficult to exploit. But protecting the natural environment has become a major trump card in today's international negotiations. The interest in ecotourism has risen, seemingly replacing cultural and other tourism as a major influence. Thinking optimistically, we may assume that every country will protect between 8 and 12 percent of its territories over the long term. But what happens if biofuels are officially endorsed, calling for the destruction of vast swaths of key tropical forests in order to plant sugarcane? Climate fluctuations that have recurred throughout geological history, and particularly the recent changes of the Quaternary Period, were clearly the basis for the upheavals in plant growth distributions. Certain zones, known as "refuges," allowed for a whole cast of species to subsist during unfavorable climatic periods. Now, moist forest refuges, for example, which are often located in hills, in mountainous regions or along riverbeds during drier periods, are being destroyed by humans as often as the vast plains regions where biodiversity is today often lower, having been repeatedly subjected to successively receding and expanding forest cover. But regardless of the way we address the problems related to Earth's future, it is certain that nearly 7 billion human beings is a lot, probably already way too many. . . .

Today, as the richer part of humanity is anxiously reviewing the dizzying progress achieved over the last century, its own ambivalent relationships with their counterparts from the south, their destructive action on most ecosystems, their impact on global climate, the depletion of fossil energy resources, and more and more other causes of concern, the idea of a free and self-contained natural world tends to offer some kind of comfort. However, things are likely to change, since recent geopolitical developments suggest that the rapid breakthrough of countries such as China, India, Russia, and Brazil will create a completely new situation.

Why do these vertical gardens I set up in different countries and different situations always produce the same impact? Maybe simply because any human being standing in front of one, whatever his or her age, sex, cultural background, or social position, will feel the breath of the wilderness in the midst of the city. The plants are truly present as if they have themselves decided to be here. What is more, they grow on a vertical substrate, and that gives us new sensations: the plants become like ourselves, developing by their own means and remaining free in front of us. All their different parts are visible: roots in the felt, basal crowns, shrub branches, slender stems of herbaceous plants, blade-supporting petioles, overall foliage, flower-bearing stems, flowers, fruits, and seeds. Seen at eye level or from underneath, plants reveal themselves. Set vertically, they can at last have a dialogue on an equal footing with human beings. Since they are obviously established in rather inaccessible places and human interventions are clearly kept to a minimum, these plants of vertical gardens appear in our eyes as free entities. The coolness and purity of the air close to a vertical garden immediately evokes mental images of tropical forests, karstic outcrops, and waterfalls. Strangely enough, even outside, in Europe's temperate climate, vertical gardens evoke tropical lushness, even though the plants on show are the same *Berberis*, *Cotoneaster*, *Campanula*, *Heuchera*, and *Polystichum* as those to be seen in any town garden.

So why do my vertical gardens evoke the tropics or even a modern-day Eden when planted in the heart of a city? This

In August 2006, during the filming of *Des racines & des ailes* (Roots and Wings), I led a team to southern Thailand, where I rediscovered *Cryptocoryne albida* in the forest streams.

In 1995 I proposed creating four botanical pillars in one of the rather empty glass stalls of the Cité des Sciences de La Villette in Paris; each column was to evoke the biodiversity of the four tropical continents – America, Africa, Asia, Oceania.

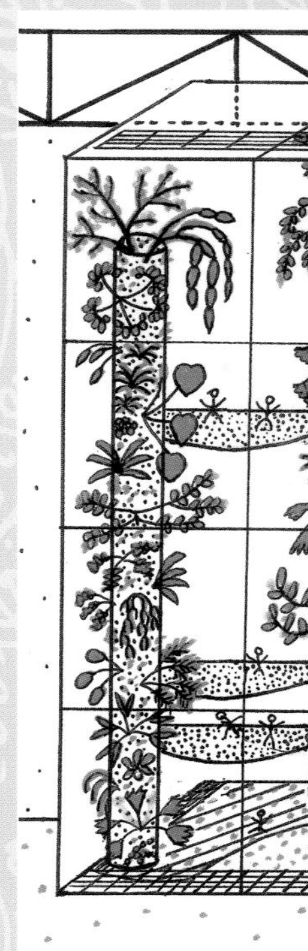

impression cannot simply be explained by the verticality of the plants, since walls covered in ivy or creepers never quite evoke that same notion of wild nature. On the contrary, these plants nourished by human hands start the conquest of their host buildings, and with impending risk. And though a bower or trellis covered in climbing plants will perhaps make us long to stretch out under its shade, it does not plunge us into a universe of untamed nature. I believe that the wide variety of plants chosen and the special sequences in which they are placed, imitating images from nature, are the reason for this near-universal reaction to vertical gardens. By integrating several hundred different species in a single wall, the imagination is fired up. In addition, it is possible to induce a positive reading of this reconstructed nature by organizing the species along slightly slanted near-vertical lines, vanishing towards the upper-right-hand section of the wall. It is apparent in nature how, on cliffs and along waterfalls, plants are distributed according to two basic patterns, depending on the substrate. If the surface is uniformly moist, a single species will tend to colonize the surface following relatively vertical lines. This is simply due to the fact that, on a favorable site, a species reproduces by shedding seeds downward. Lateral spreading is usually through stolons or basal suckers. On rocks exposed to wind and sunlight, however, plants settle in oblique or horizontal crevices in the geological substrate where there is water and a little humus. Those images from Japanese or Chinese prints bear no resemblance to vertical gardens since there are large areas of rock denuded of plant life. So it is most likely, in choosing a wide variety of plants capable of cohabitating over the long-term and setting them up relatively vertically with all of their organs visible, that this recognizable image of the vertical garden has established itself.

Besides the installations that I made at home and in the apartments of a few friends, my first public vertical garden was created for the Cité des Sciences et de l'Industrie in Paris, following a meeting with Gilles Clément and Philippe Niez in 1986. It was a beautiful installation, but there was no hint of reaction. That was not a problem for me since I was heavily committed to research for my state thesis. It was also starting in 1986 that I became deeply involved in the *Radeau des Cimes* (Canopy Raft) expeditions, alongside Gilles Ebersolt, Dany Cleyet-Marrel, and Francis Hallé (whom I had had the good fortune of meeting in 1976 at the University of Kuala Lumpur during my first long stay in Malaysia for my graduate thesis). That allowed me to expand my research into strategies for plant growth in highly luminous areas (in this particular case, the tips of the topmost tree branches in a canopy) and compare this with the shade-tolerant plants of the understory, which receive only 1 percent of the light that reaches the canopy. In this way I was able to show that the plant's architectural complexity (overall shape, leaf structure and dimensions, effective branching, biomechanical balance, vegetative propagation, floral and perifloral structures) was a lot more elaborate and diversified in the understory than in the canopy. This is probably mainly due to the absence of wind, the only slight variations in temperature and humidity, and the lack of competition in the understory. When you look at a vertical garden, you get the impression of nature returning to the city by the way its architecture is tiered from forest canopy to understory, or from the cliff's edge to the dark recesses at its base: the simplest shapes with the greatest number of branches are located in the open, windswept tops. As the eye descends toward the protected, shaded zones, it finds an increasing number of various shapes and rather sophisticated leaf structures, such as you might find in Saxifragaceae, Urticaceae, *Epimedium*, or countless ferns.

It was not until in 1991 that I mounted my first outdoor vertical garden, in a new habitat in the Paris suburbs. Upon seeing a horrible concrete wall in the courtyard outside the window of the main room, I realized that I needed to take the plunge and start incorporating "outdoor" plants into my plans: after twenty years of being immersed in tropical plants, I thus decided that temperate plants must be equally adaptable to vertical gardens outside the home. I was not familiar with this temperate world, since the flora of France and Europe was largely unknown to me, unlike the flora of North America, the Himalayas, and the temperate Far East, which I had encountered in botanical gardens. Yet I already knew that a vertical garden set up outside would not present any fundamentally different constraints in terms of its structure. On the other hand, the light source was different: instead of receiving artificial light, as is usually the case for indoor gardens, an outdoor garden gets light from the sun. That means that the choice of species depends on where this new vertical garden is situated: oriented toward the east, it gets the morning sunlight on its upper reaches, while the base remains shaded. Sun-loving shrubs of cliffs and embankments (*Buddleja, Cotoneaster, Hypericum . . .*) were placed at the top, while the lower, shaded parts welcomed *Heuchera, Tiarella, Carex, Polystichum,* or even *Iris japonica*, which became one of my fetish plants after seeing it on hillsides and along waterfalls in Japan's forest understories. Straight away, the plants developed perfectly well on these prototype walls, which did not surprise me too much since I had had nearly twenty years of satisfactory results indoors with vertical tropical gardens, whose origins dated back to my first trip in Asia in 1972.

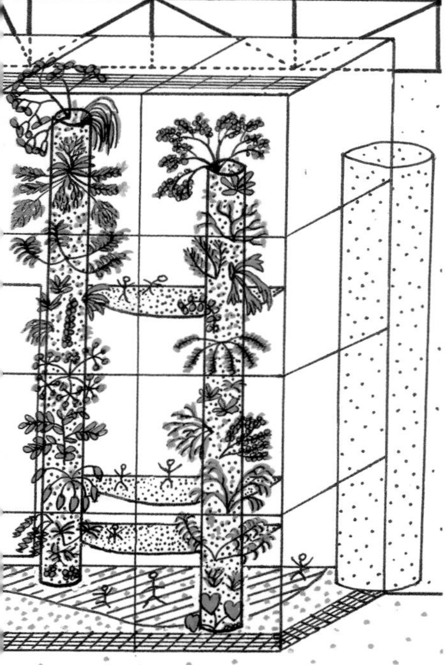

Cité des Sciences et de l'Industrie, Paris

A fine adventure for the Green Bridge of the Cité des Sciences de La Villette: our 1986 mission to Guadeloupe gave us the opportunity to collect some Araceae and Cyclanthaceae with Alain Rousteau from the Office National des Forêts (he is currently a university professor in Pointe-à-Pitre). Panels attached to each surface anticipated my later green blades.

first attempts on the terrace

One of my signature species, *Iris japonica*. It has been difficult for me to imagine a vertical garden without it since seeing it blanket the glistening rocks of the understory in Japan and China, creating long vertical corridors of green hands welcoming visitors.

From the shaded banks in the heart of Kanazawa's mountains to the vertical garden in Créteil, the same waterfall of green locks dangle from *Carex nachiana*. As always, many species from the Far East adorn my Créteil garden.

Under a *Pandanus helicopus* in Khao Sok in southern Thailand.

That first outdoor vertical garden therefore came quite a bit later than my tropical indoor gardens and only dates back about fifteen years. However, it was the basis for my success with vertical gardens. When that wall was about two years old, my friend Eric Ossart, who was in charge of selecting the plant species for the newly created international festival on gardens and landscapes in Chaumont-sur-Loire, felt that Jean-Paul Pigeat, the festival's founder and director, might be interested in my work for their third festival in the summer of 1994, with its theme of acclimatization. Jean-Paul was immediately enthusiastic and not only proposed that I present my vertical gardens but also accepted my suggestion to set up an expedition to Chile to look for new species that would be adaptable to our climate. Chile was particularly interesting to my research on forest understory plants since I had come to feel that those shade-loving plants of the southern hemisphere's humid, temperate forests had garnered little attention or were a bit underrepresented in terms of their species. That expedition confirmed that understory angiosperms (flowering plants) are only significantly present in the understory as shrubby species (*Azara, Berberis, Drimys, Fuchsia, Lomatia, Chusquea*), while herbaceous plants are surprisingly rare (a few *Pilea, Ourisia, Calceolaria*). On the other hand, there were numerous types of ferns present, shaping the understory landscape. Just a few months ago I came to the same conclusion in another temperate region of the southern hemisphere, namely the understory of southeast Australia. We can postulate that these temperate rainforests in the southern hemisphere, with their rather restricted distribution, offered only limited opportunities for refuges during the Quaternary Period's drier climatic phases, and that the shade-tolerant herbaceous species, which were generally more vulnerable than the shrubby species due to their lack of food reserves in the stems and to their rather undeveloped root system, must have successively disappeared. Their disappearance would have been all the more pronounced given their usual method of dispersing seeds at only short distances. Ferns, though equally fragile, are capable of recolonizing quite rapidly areas that once again become damp and favorable starting with a rather limited number of individual plants, thanks to the millions of spores transported great distances along the lightest of winds.

And so, the meeting with Jean-Paul Pigeat initiated a new way for me to approach the plant world. As for the vertical gardens, Jean-Paul asked an architect friend, Michel Mangematin, to help me organize their layout and design in the space allocated to me in Chaumont. Thanks to the Chaumont festival, I became part of the group connected to new trends and creations in the world of gardens. I was no longer considered a mere researcher isolated in his laboratory or apartment carrying out experiments that were deemed interesting only to a limited number of people. Through Chaumont, my work became ordinary, in the best sense of that word. Enthusiasts, architects, designers, and urban planners alike realized the potential for my gardens within their own projects. I would never had imagined, before Chaumont, that I would become so intensely involved in contemplating urban evolution in relation to nature.

Immediately after Chaumont, Jacqueline Nebout proposed creating a garden for the Parc Floral in Paris. That garden in particular underscores the questions related to water purification by plants since it has only ever been irrigated with water from the duck pond below it, without any added nutritive solution. Working on the project was like being ten years old again, when I used to read that *Philodendron* roots purified aquarium water.

Jean Nouvel was the first architect to become interested in my work, starting in 1996. At that time we began preparing for the competition for the French embassy in Berlin, integrating the collection and distribution of rainwater in order to irrigate the garden. But we did not win. Afterwards we organized a few projects with Australia that were not completed. Fortunately we have since worked in close collaboration for projects in Seoul, Barcelona, and Paris (the Quai Branly Museum), and several new projects are in the works.

It was in the world of contemporary art that I was able to carry out new creations following the Chaumont festival. In 1997 I was invited by the Contemporary Art Center in Albi as part of their "In situ, in visu" exhibition. I was given carte blanche and I decided to present two pieces with unusual plant structures. One was a Green Blade measuring only 1 inch (2 cm) thick, covered in plants on both sides (I have since developed other green blades in New York, Kanazawa, and Saõ Paulo). The other piece was an oddly shaped, artificial boulder partially covered in plants. This second structure was constructed of resin-coated polystyrene covered in sand, and it resembled the rough rocks found in the understory. It was a new type of garden, without irrigation cloth. I have made others since, such as at the Roche-Guyon chateau, the new CFDT headquarters in Paris, and as part of a collective research project for the Ministry of Culture. The contemporary art world has the advantage of being open to all new and experimental proposals.

The following year I participated in the exhibition "Être nature" (To Be Nature) at the Cartier Foundation for Contemporary Art. It was an interesting work, but was not fully understood. In fact, tired of hearing repeated assertions that humid tropical zones offer a much broader biodiversity than the more impoverished temperate zones, I decided to provoke the question by presenting two pieces. One, outside, included a wide variety of species and plant shapes from temperate areas. Inside, the companion wall presented a structural and specific limitations for tropical areas. As I expected, the inside piece aroused less interest, while the exterior garden was a great success and everyone opposed its dismantling at the end of the exhibition. It is still there more than ten years later! I was then invited to the exhibition "Le temps déborde" (Time Spills Over) at the Blanc-Mesnil Cultural Forum outside Paris. I presented a vertical garden around a large round bay window several yards in diameter inscribed inside a square. The inside was also covered in tropical species.

The idea of making buildings transparent or invisible among plants related to what I had always been creating at home. Immersed in a tropical universe, I try to forget the seasons and to create continuity between indoors and out, especially in winter. That is why I use so many evergreens in my outdoor gardens, generally within the sightline from inside. Fortunately, certain species, particularly of flora from the understory in southeast China and Japan, grow equally well indoors with temperatures ranging from 68° to 72° F (20° to 22° C) as they do outdoors in temperatures getting down to 15° F (−10° C). These include *Saxifraga stolonifera, Ardisia crenata* and *A. crispa, Pilea petiolaris, Ficus repens, Aspidistra elatior, Liriope,* and *Ophiopogon*, to name a few. The effect is always breathtaking when, in the month of January, you see the same broad leaves of an *Aspidistra* covered in snow outside and basking in the dry warmth inside the apartment, separated merely by a sheet of glass! I have always tried to deny winter, and I often go out in cold weather dressed in only a T-shirt and shorts, with flip-flops on my feet. Of course, the way I live my life is not always fully applicable to my plant creations, and I keep the climate fully in mind when selecting species.

The contemporary art world has always been supportive of my work. One of my most renowned installations has been the Green Bridge (in fact, a green blade) at the 21st Century Museum of Contemporary Art in Kanazawa, Japan. As a resident artist in New Delhi, I was able to cover the four pillars of the reception room in the French embassy and free Bengali birds that I had purchased in the Old Delhi market. They now crisscross the room, flying from pillar to pillar. One of my last pieces was the Green Vortex installed in July 2007 at Lacoste as part of an exhibition with the Savannah College of Art and Design. It was in 2007, during my exhibition "Folies végétales" (Plant follies), at the Espace EDF Electra in Paris, that the public had a chance to discover the connections between my research in botany and my work on transposing plants inside human spaces.

It has only been for about ten years that vertical gardens have existed as a solution for urban planners, architects, museographers, interior designers, and developers. The year 1998 saw the first projects created for museum spaces, starting with the walls of the aquarium in Genoa, Italy, and of the Végétarium in Gacilly. After a short break between installations (including an interesting project for the experimental garden at the Méry-sur-Oise chateau), it was Andrée Putman who allowed me to take a decisive leap forward with Pershing Hall in 2001. Andrée was quite familiar with my vertical gardens at my home in Créteil, and she loved them. But she had understood that what she saw covering a few yards of space could be recreated over 100 feet (30 m). My prior projects had all ended up being up to about 33 feet (10 m) high. The tallest at the time were the vertical gardens at Blanc-Mesnil and on Saint-Germain island in Issy-les-Moulineaux. I was not worried about the height (I am currently working on several projects, to be tall towers 820 to 985 feet (250 to 300 m), but I needed someone else convinced as well! The change in scale that Andrée was proposing is of great importance to a biologist, since what is true and possible on one scale may not be possible on another. The wall at Pershing Hall had broad repercussions, probably because it was the first time I was creating a direct link with urban architecture, covering the high walls of a traditional Parisian building with plants.

And finally, a last essential event along this odyssey of vertical gardens: the Quai Branly Museum with Jean Nouvel, inaugurated in June of 2006 by the president of France.

Façade of the Quai Branly Museum, May 2006

At the origin of it all was the aquarium. The first one that I installed in my parents' apartment must date back nearly forty years! At the age of sixteen, I plunged *Monstera* cuttings in my first large aquarium, which held more than 80 gallons (300 l) of water, so that their roots absorbed the excess nitrates, purifying the water and creating a healthier environment for the fish. Today, my aquarium holds about 260 gallons (1,000 l), but is now laced with Araceae: instead of *Monstera deliciosa*, with its oversize leaves, I installed *Epipremnum aureum* from the Solomon Islands (often called *Pothos*) and *Philodendron billietae* from French Guiana. The long white roots overlap and create shelter for the fish, as do the numerous underwater plants, which include *Aponogeton rigidifolius*, *Cryptocoryne cordata*, *Barclaya longifolia*, *Nymphaea micrantha*, *Hygrophila balsamica*, and *Ammannia gracilis*. Below the aquarium, lamps light up small tubs of wading Korean frogs (*Bombina orientalis*), which have been reproducing there for about twenty years. There are three layers extending from floor to ceiling: a sort of forest edge overrun by climbing Araceae, a stream you can easily plunge your hands into, and finally a kind of cave before which one must kneel in order to discover the plants and animals inhabiting it. As for my desk, it is located in an open room between the vertical garden and the aquarium. Birds fly overhead from one space to the other, and I work under Zarah Leander's protective gaze.

I have always refused to heed the limits between inside and outside imposed by a human lifestyle that migrated from tropical origins to colder, even glacial, climates. To heighten the absurdity, life in tropical cities requires air-conditioning to cool the atmosphere: it is true that within tropical forests, the temperature is mild and rarely exceeds 75°F (25° C), whereas it regularly reaches 95°F (35° C) in cities, which are generally located on former forested lands. Thus, wherever one goes in the world, regardless of the season, it is necessary to either heat or cool dwellings. We are happily moving toward architecture with progressively better thermal balance. The vertical garden is part of that process, with its metal frame generating an air buffer, and its expanded PVC layer, its irrigation cloth, and of course the plants themselves. My refusal to dissociate my home's inside from its outside is marked by a continuous flow of plants on either side of the window: a mere tenth of an inch (3 mm) of glass separates the *Philodendron goeldii* from the *Tropaeolum ciliatum* and *Mucuna sempervirens* that hide the sad thujas outside. Across from the window, the gabled wall is covered with a vertical garden composed primarily of evergreens. Inside, I have gradually allowed the *Philodendron goeldii*, which was grown from a seed brought back from French Guiana in 1978, to be slowly taken over by a *Pandanus* that we harvested with Pascal Héni in 1999 from elephant dung in Khao Sok National Park in southern Thailand. I didn't realize at the time that this *Pandanus helicopus* was going to become a tree!

All my new experiments are of course tested at home. It was Pascal's idea to layer a small, 20-inch (50-cm) fountain with an irrigation cloth and allow moss to grow. Under the light of a small halogen projector, different species of Cyanophyceae (blue algae) and Chlorophyceae (green algae) developed spontaneously. A few weeks later, *Bryophyta* started growing among the algae filaments, gradually covering them over. Two years later, the same moss population (still impossible to determine, since I am waiting for the sporogonia to form) is still covering this structure, evoking a miniature cliff. Below them, just to the left, rocks placed in a small aquarium, covered with mosses, begonias, and ferns, were a first step toward the Along Bay that I presented in Espace EDF Electra. As for the unused bidet, I transformed it into an Asian understory swamp with Java moss (*Taxiphyllum barbieri*) covering the basin walls and several species of *Cryptocoryne* carpeting its sandy bottom. A few years ago, I developed a piece for a charity, at Gérard Garouste's request. In a small box with limited dimensions I created a minuscule vertical garden adorned with *Ludisia*, *Elatostema,* and *Cryptanthus,* among others. But the confined and overheated atmosphere did not allow the plants to thrive….

On the vertical garden in the yard around my house I conduct my experiments, especially for trying out new species. For example, on the heels of my first trip to Japan with Jean-Paul Pigeat I decided to install some *Iris japonica* on my vertical gardens, after having seen them dangle from the banks and wet rocks of the understory. That is how I came to understand why in gardens their leaves were always fraying at the tips that touched the ground. In nature the angle of their substrate is such that the leaves never touch the ground, and remain intact. I also tested out my cherished, cold-resistant Urticaceae, such as *Boehmeria tricuspis, Pilea petiolaris, Elatostema umbellatum,* and *Debregeasia edulis,* in my gardens at home. The results of these attempts are generally satisfactory, since I only install species that grow vertically or on steep inclines in nature. There are sometimes a few surprises. *Kerria japonica,* which I have always seen on slopes and cliffs in China and Japan, often had difficulty growing in my gardens, and I wasn't able to figure out why. But that mystery adds to the magic of a never-ending quest.

Structure, installation and maintenance

Is it really necessary to expound at length on the way to attach a floor cloth to a plastic board, with a hose connected at the top?

More than twenty years of experiments have gradually led me towards simplest structural solution, as I mentioned in my patent entitled "Design for growing plants without soil on a vertical surface." In that document, I simply outline that one requires a "structure consisting of a vertical surface covered in felt, which replaces the soil and retains water. The plants are attached to that layer of felt so that the roots latch on to its surface.... The vertical surface consists of a vertical panel of some solid, rigid, and waterproof material that is also both nontoxic and rot-proof. The felt is attached with staples or glue.... The felt is synthetic.... The structure includes an automatic humidification system regulated by a clock in order to moisten the felt.... There is a tray to collect the water...."

Thanks to recommendations sent by the INPI (National Institute for Industrial Property) following each patent request, I realized that what I was proposing was something quite new because the plant roots would be developing on a surface (felt, i.e., irrigation cloth) and no longer inside a volume, as is the case with countless other systems of "soil-less" cultivation, where roots develop inside substrates (clay balls, peat chunks, peat moss, mineral wool, coconut fibers, polystyrene mixes), which tend to be at least ¾ inch (2 cm) thick. The difference may seem trivial but the weight of a vertical installation is crucial, considering a 1/10 or 0,1-inch (3-mm) support weighs only about 6.5 pounds per square yard (3 kg per m^2) when wet, while a ¾-inch (2-cm) substrate weighs 44 pounds (20 kg) and a 4-inch (10-cm) substrate weighs 220 pounds (100 kg)! In addition, a thinner material, like this cloth, will not be subject to settling over time, nor will it be deformed by changes in temperature. The micro-gaps between the fibers dilate in frost conditions without changing their overall structure, precisely because it is not a woven material and is therefore unstructured. The solidity of the material is reinforced by a woven polypropylene film placed between the cloth and the expanded-PVC boards. The material does not rot because it is made of recovered bits of broken-down acrylic textiles. Of all of the vertical garden's elements, this irrigation cloth is the only one that affects the plant's biology: it is in those fibers that the roots develop, allowing the plant to hold long-term as well as to absorb water and nutrients. In fact, the highly water-conducting irrigation cloth is quite comparable to a thin layer of algae, moss, and hepatics covering forest rocks, tree trunks, and branches. Any saxicolous or epiphyte species installed in a vertical garden will root into the cloth in exactly the same manner it would in a bed of moss on a rocky surface. In order to make plant installation easier, the cloth is made up of two layers attached by rust-proof steel staples to the sturdy PVC structure. The first layer is slit open with a cutter to create horizontal openings a few inches (5 to 10 cm) long, depending on the plant's dimensions. The plants are removed from most of the soil and their roots inserted between the two layers. Staples on either side of the plant's base hold it in place initially. Later, the roots start to radiate from the plant and progressively work their way into the cloth in all directions. Thanks to these roots, as they weave into the cloth as well as under the staples, the plants can fully attach themselves and survive in a vertical garden over time. The roots of certain shrubs reach up to several yards long, with nothing impeding their growth. The completely open structure, limited only by its edges, allows shrubs and small herbaceous plants to coexist with no competition at the root level because the cloth is able to evenly distribute water and nutrients across its entire surface and therefore to every root. The plants are not restricted in their root growth as they would be in containers or box systems piled on top of each other.

All of the exchange between plant, water, and atmosphere takes place through the irrigation cloth. All research on soil biology has signaled the important interactions between microorganisms and plants, the best-known example being mycorrhiza, which are complex associations (internal or external depending on the species) between fungus and roots, allowing for increased absorption of water and mineral salts into the roots. In fact, the fungus hyphae develop much more extensively than root hairs. The mycorrhiza play a larger role in groups of woody plants (trees and shrubs) than groups of herbaceous plants. Beyond these more or less tight associations of fungi and plant roots, other microorganisms such as various types of bacteria or cyanobacteria live in narrow association with plant roots, often forming modules, as is the case with legumes, Cycadales, alders, and *Ceanothus*. As a general rule, these microorganisms connected to plant roots develop better when the substrate is well oxygenated, as is the case in a vertical garden because the irri-

For the vertical garden at Madrid's Caixa Forum we used a wide platform for the installation of twenty thousand plants belonging to three hundred different species.

gation cloth is in direct contact with the oxygen in the air. The microorganisms that grow in contact with plant roots arouse everyone's interest these days since they have the reputation, bolstered by a number of studies, of being able to transform more or less toxic organic molecules (including pesticides and volatile organic compounds, or VOCs) emitted by industry, vehicles, and biological activity of humans and animals. In cities, of course, various types of dust are added to this chemical pollution. Electrostatic forces attract dust to city plant leaves, and during the dry season, tree leaves in large cities in the tropics are often completely covered in a black, greasy film. These residues are ultimately washed away and dissolved by the rain. In a vertical garden, the leaf surface as well as the entire surface of the felt trap this dust. Once trapped, the dust is decomposed by the water and microorganisms into chemical elements that the plants can more easily absorb. In addition, various tars and microfragments of rubber from tire wear along the major roadways are carried away in puddle spray and may deposit on the lower sections of a vertical garden's irrigation cloth, only to be decomposed and assimilated by the plant roots. The irrigation cloth may absorb wastewater and act as a mechanical filter comparable to the filtering matter used to rid water of suspended minerals and organic matter. But unlike filtering compartments, which require regular cleaning, the irrigation cloth is capable of blocking and then quickly mineralizing these elements through air contact, making them absorbable by the roots. This has been the case with the vertical garden in the Parc Floral in Paris for the past twelve years and with the one on my home for twenty-five years; the cloth has never had to be cleaned. The irrigation cloth thus becomes a micro-ecosystem that recycles, through biological processes, the elements it incorporates, whether from the system itself (dead roots replaced by new ones) or from the outside (dust particles, puddle splash water, suspended matter in the water, pollutants and other volitile organic compounds).

The cloth is irrigated through a simple plastic tube, often made of low-density polyurethane in order to tolerate any expansion caused by freezing water. The tube is placed horizontally across the top of the vertical garden and 1⁄12-inch (2-mm) holes are pierced every 4 inches (10 cm). Thanks to sufficient water pressure (roughly 3 bars, a standard water pressure for apartment buildings) along piping segments no longer than about 10 yards, watering occurs three to five times a day, depending on the season and the vertical garden's exposure. Each watering lasts for one to three minutes (on rare occasion, five) depending on the height to be irrigated. In order to maintain a mineral balance throughout the root systems, a highly dilute nutritive solution (between 0.03 and 0.09 ounce per fluid ounce or 0,2 to 0,3 gram per liter), about ten times less than tends to be used in horticulture and agriculture, is distributed with the help of a mechanical dispenser. When the irrigation water is collected from rainfall on roofs and terraces, the concentration is even lower because that water lacks calcium carbonate (lime) that partially prevents useful ions from being absorbed. Of course, when an aquarium is installed as the reservoir, or a pool or wastewater, no nutritive solution is required. Depending upon sun and wind exposure, time of year, and type of water recycling (quite desirable!), a vertical garden requires daily 1–10 pints per square yard (.5–5 liters of water per square meter per day). Outdoors, in a temperate climate, proper water management will require around 3 quarts per square yard (3 liters per square meter) in the summer while the amount is rarely more than a quart (liter) for an interior garden sheltered from the wind. These average amounts are quite low compared to what is used for watering gardens and urban parks.

The irrigation cloth cannot stand in the air all alone, like a botanical sail: the force of the wind, the weight of the plants, their various layouts and types of water distribution would not allow it. I had thus from the beginning planned a support structure: the support was to consist of a vertical panel made of rigid, solid, waterproof, nontoxic, and rot-proof material.

In the beginning I used wood panels in an attempt to recreate the epiphytes' natural supporting structure – forest tree trunks. The panels were made of wood fragments pressed together into chipboard. To ensure that the material would last, I selected what is known as marine chipboards, which is meant to be water-resistant. In fact, even with regular watering, this material lasts three to five years without deteriorating. After that, it crumbles, pulling down the irrigation cloth and plants. In order to meet the material requirements I had laid out, I decided to explore various plastics. After testing several materials, it seemed that expanded PVC had the advantage of being light, with a density of 0.7, which means that a 1⁄3-inch-thick sheet weighs only 15 pounds per square yard (a 10-mm sheet weighs only 7 kg per m^2). In addition, unlike other hard plastics, this micro-honeycombed material resists cracking under the action of a staple gun. With Staples that are only 1⁄3 inch (10 mm) long, it can withstand a mechanical force of nearly 1,500 pounds per square inch (100kg/cm^2), which is well beyond the pressure exerted by the larger shrubs in a vertical garden, even during a storm. During the December 1999 gale, two large oaks fell close to the three freestanding vertical gardens in Chaumont-sur-Loire, but not a single plant or an edge of irrigation cloth was torn from the garden. The range of structures capable of supporting an irrigation cloth will grow over time and current progress is such in the plastics industry that, in the near future, materials that are newer and more environmentally friendly than expanded PVC will be created, offering the same desired qualities. Other types of recycled plastic have already been tried out for certain of my vertical gardens, for example, in Japan.

The rigid panel of expanded PVC can obviously be affixed directly to the support wall for the vertical garden, but I recommend allowing for air to circulate between the two structures in order to let the supporting wall "breathe." That is why, among various possible solutions, a metal tube gridwork (aluminum, galvanized steel, or stainless steel) is usually installed on the bearing wall. It is generally a square-mesh metal frame made of square-cut tubes 1½ inches (4 cm) thick, with a mesh size of 23.8 inches (61 cm) simply because the PVC panels come sized 47.6 x 95.2 inches (1.22 x 2.44 m). Sometimes builders prefer simply to install vertical tubes with

Installation of the vertical garden's support structure and plants as well as subsequent upkeep requires either scaffolding or an elevating work platform depending on the location.

In order to install the wide strips of plants at Siam Paragon, the scaffolding is constructed of metal rods and not of bamboo as one still frequently sees in the provinces.

Installation of the metal frame for the Forum Culturel in Blanc-Mesnil: a simple mesh constructed with rust-proof steel tubing, ready to support the expanded PVC panels and the irrigation cloth. The empty space between the expanded PVC and the building's wall can be filled with insulating material.

In 1994, in Chaumont-sur-Loire, I myself planted thousands of plants for three vertical gardens with a tapestry stapler. My friend Pascal Héni helped me, and what blisters we got on our hands! Since then, Sylvain Bidaut has been in charge of the installation teams, and the staplers are now pneumatic.

For each installation, we must stock the plants we receive, the equivalent of about thirty plants per square yard. For example, a small vertical garden measuring 33 feet (10 m) high and wide requires the storage and maintenance of about 3,000 plants before they are installed.

A simple polyurethane tube with 1/10-inch (2-mm) holes every 4 inches (10 cm) allows water to be distributed evenly over the irrigation cloth, which is made of recycled polyamide fibers. The structure and irrigation system of the Chaumont-sur-Loire vertical gardens were set up by Bruno Hyvernaud. He has since then fitted several dozens more in Europe.

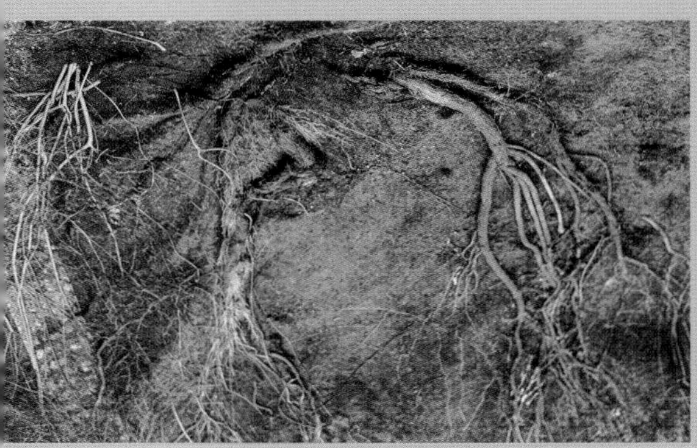

During installation, there is a range of reactions to the irrigation cloth: some find it hideous, some find it to be quite kitsch, while for others it is reminiscent of granite rock surface. In fact, the sheets of polyamide fabric present a curious shade of deep pink that disappears quite quickly when the algae, mosses, and microorganisms begin to cover its surface and crevices under the intermittent irrigation provided by the piping installed at top.

The irrigation cloth's compact polyamide fibers resemble a stone-covering moss carpet: this 1/10-inch (3-mm) thick synthetic, rot-proof fibrous material is crisscrossed with the roots of plants. Algae, moss and microorganisms grow in this perfectly oxygenated substrate, breaking down larger organic molecules into simple elements that can easily be absorbed by the roots. This cleansing action includes the physical trapping of particles (dust, water-borne particles) by the wet fibers of the irrigation cloth as well as the trapping and chemical degradation of the volatile organic compounds.

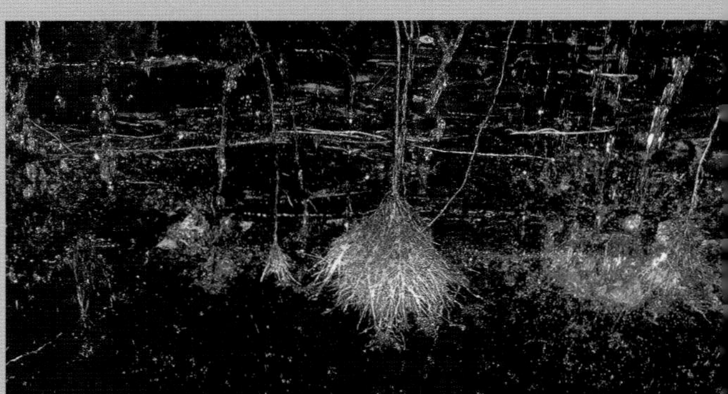

At the base of the irrigation cloth, the roots can be plunged into a ditch or tub where they grow by branching out, as they would in an aquarium or in natural pools at the base of a waterfall.

horizontal bars attached where the PVC panels join, these being riveted to the metal tubes. A waterproof seal is necessary along those joints: the builders use a silicone seal covered with an adhesive strip, like those used for sealing terraces and other surfaces.

The total weight of the vertical garden remains pretty low: at 14.4 pounds per square foot (7 kg per m^2) of expanded PVC panels ⅓ inch (10 mm) thick, you add 6 to 10 pound per square foot (3 to 5 kg per m^2) for the irrigation cloth, depending on the quantity of water it encloses and 2 to 10 pound per square foot (1 to 5 kg per m^2) for the plants, depending on the species. That makes an average of about 30 pounds per square yard (15 kg per m^2) for this structure that promotes the growth and long-term stability of the vertical garden's plants. We should keep in mind the weight of the metal frame, which varies considerably according to structure and type of metal. Even with the heaviest metal frame, the total weight for the vertical garden doesn't surpass 100 pounds per square foot (50 kg per m^2) and can remain as low as 40 pounds (20 kg) if the connecting structure between the vertical garden and the bearing wall is light.

The plants, the irrigation cloth, the ⅓-inch (1-cm) thick PVC panels, and the 1½-inch (4-cm) gap created by the metal supportive structure produce solid insulation between the building and the outdoors, against the cold of winter as well as the heat of summer. But it helps to use traditional materials for heat and sound insulation in the small space between the bearing wall and the vertical garden. In this way, a vertical garden may be used to renovate run-down apartment building, conferring insulation, visual comfort, and better air quality.

My vertical gardens, which can now be seen nearly worldwide, seem so simple, so natural, and perhaps even a little self-evident; I think this is simply because I have had the opportunity to immerse myself in the plant world for a good forty years. How could I dissociate my empirical, scientific, and artistic approaches? It seems to me that they came in succession, and continue to overlap to this day. As I write at a hotel in Honolulu on Christmas Eve, 2007, I look forward to spending an entire week in the forest of Kauai, the most ancient island in the Hawaiian archipelago. My research will focus on the *Cyanea, Clermontia*, and other endemic *Cyrtandra* growing in the forest understory, sometimes as epiphytes, as well as along cliff waterfalls. I will test my hypotheses on the relations between the modes of plant evolution in the understory and the means of seed dispersion, rooting structures for seedlings, and the overall shapes of plants in this insular environment. We will also be investigating new areas of volcanic relief colonized by species with which I am yet unfamiliar. It is this plant diversity that allows me to create unique vertical gardens each time. Even when I install the same species, the life conditions are different on each wall, in dimensions, in exposure, in temperature, in water quality. Using several hundred species on a single large garden promises a variety of visual aspects and has the incalculable advantage of preventing disease propagation and insect infestations, as is the case with most diversified ecosystems. I have never had to use any treatment on my outdoor vertical gardens. Inside, without wind and rain, a few scale insects may appear and can be taken care of with an application of mild pesticide, though they also may be removed merely with a solid spray of warm water (95° to 100° F [35° to 38° C]), unless there are insect-eating birds around, as there are at my house.

In order to create the plant sequences for each project, meaning the order, placement, and blend of each species, I rely on several criteria, the most important being the geographic location of the vertical garden, its latitude, and its cardinal orientation. A vertical garden installed in Seoul will naturally require different species than a vertical garden in New York, Miami, Paris, Barcelona, Bangkok, or Dubai. On the other hand, for gardens created inside buildings, the climate is relatively stable worldwide, regardless of latitude. The comfort zone for humans is a temperature of roughly 68° F (20° C). That constant temperature is comparable to the average temperatures in the understory of tropical forests at altitudes under 2,000 to 2,600 feet (600 to 800 m). Even though exposure to natural light, or to artificial lighting installed on the vertical garden, approaches the levels reached in the understory (about 1,500 to 2,000 lux, or 1.5 to 2 percent of full sunlight), the case is not the same for relative humidity: in apartments, offices, and shopping centers, relative humidity rarely exceeds 50 percent, whereas it gets up to 85 to 95 percent in the tropical rainforest understory.

The low relative humidity is detrimental to the growth and survival of many fragile understory species because their delicate leaves are not adapted to the dryness of the atmosphere, as is the case for example with several *Sonerila, Phyllagathis, Henckelia, Pilea,* and numerous species of ferns. Fortunately, a vertical garden creates its own microclimate in relation to the relative humidity. Measurements recorded at a distance of 2 inches (5 cm) from the cloth showed a relative humidity reaching 90 percent, decreasing rapidly with more distance: it reaches 80 percent between 4 and 8 inches (10 and 20 cm), 70 percent between 12 and 20 inches (30 and 50 cm), dropping to only 60 to 65 percent 3 feet (1 m) away from the cloth and leveling out at ambient humidity less than 60 inches (1.5 m) away. The constantly moist surface of the cloth, as well as water from the plants' transpiration and respiration, improves the living conditions considerably for the plants installed in a vertical garden, allowing for the use of fragile species that would not survive in ordinary containers. The microorganisms can only prosper in the cloth's fiber thanks to that humidity, and we should keep in mind their role in purifying the air.

Once the climatic conditions are considered for each location, it is necessary to know which plant species will be available; the range of diversity varies considerably from one country to another. In Western Europe, for example, there is an extensive number of species

We always put a scaffolding in place in order to build the metal structure, attach the PVC panels, staple the irrigation cloth, install the irrigation system, and place the plants.

A few months after installation, the plants have covered the house. On both sides of the narrow windows, the PVC panels are made watertight at their edges with a silicone-based glue and adhesive stripping normally used for terraces.

You can't see it, but even the roof is covered in plants by the same process, but my choice there has been for *Aubrieta, Cerastium, Delosperma, Iberis, Sedum*….

A private home in Belgium

It was by chance one evening that I met Carine and David at some friends' place in Brussels. Without knowing who I was, they told me about their project to cover their house entirely with plants and the difficulties they had encountered. When I told them who I was, they considered me almost as a savior! Afterward we had several meetings with Philippe Samyn, the architect who had designed their stunning house. I was very interested because it was my first opportunity to design a rooftop garden and to envelop an entire house. After much discussion about design and budget with Philippe Samyn, David, and Carine, the construction of the vertical garden was ready in the spring of 2006 and the planting took place in June. Designing the plant sequences was exciting because we had to keep in mind the various exposures of each side and the paths that the inhabitants would take. Enveloping a house with plants before the main construction was even finished posed a few problems, but after a year of readjustments, everything worked out smoothly. What also interested me about this job was that the water distributed to the plants was rainwater collected along the roof edges; some additional water came from a well. Any runoff is recycled, as at the Parc Floral in Paris, and a frost-proof waterway encircles the house.

These ice-covered *Ophiopogon* are waiting to thaw. Several vertical gardens have survived temperatures reaching down to 5°F (-15° C).

registered in greenhouses and nurseries. Research in various catalogs shows that more than fifty thousand different plants (species and cultivars) are available. In the United States, a few nurseries offer a wide selection of species but individual plants are available in relatively low numbers. Few species are cultivated in great numbers and they are often referred to by their common names. In the Far East (China, Japan, Korea, Taiwan, Hong Kong), numerous species are available, but finding the nurseries is a challenge. What a pleasure to meet an old gentleman cultivating side-by-side with the same care different Omoto (*Rohdea japonica*) varieties, some only worth about a dollar and others fetching nearly $1,500! What a change from our calibrated systems for growing plants, where price is factored into greenhouse heating costs. In other countries where I have installed vertical gardens, the choice of species was more limited – in India for example. In fact, in that huge country, many nurseries are located around Bangalore and the supply in Delhi is highly seasonal, so much so that in winter I had only fifty species to choose from for the French Embassy's columnar gardens. In Bangkok, a city I've known for thirty-five years, the variety of cultivated species is probably the highest I've encountered. In the gigantic market at Chatuchak, dedicated to plant vendors on Wednesdays and Thursdays, nearly five thousand different species and cultivars are available. In Thailand, it is not the art of the garden that is of interest, but the plants as individuals, which obviously accords with my own perspective on the plant world in its relation to humans. Depending on the site or country, the range of species that I could install on a vertical garden is practically limitless.

All the selected species in each project are arranged into plant sequences, which are designed based on the climatic conditions of the different areas on the vertical garden, the rates of growth, and the esthetic and structural aspects of each species. In the case of an outdoor vertical garden, I try to recreate the plant gradient observed along a cliff face, from the top exposed to full sun and wind, down to its rocky base, which is often plunged in understory and sheltered from the wind and strong fluctuations in temperature and humidity. For an indoor vertical garden I prefer the gradient that runs from the forest canopy, with its array of hemi-epiphytes and epiphytes, down to the understory, with saxicolous species confined to rocks and other species to river banks.

As a general rule, and it is this aspect that defines the vertical garden, I install large shrubby species in the upper sections and smaller herbaceous species below. You therefore confront gradation that is the reverse of what you typically see on garden walls where the largest plant volume remains at the base. Beyond recreating a natural layout, having the larger volumes above and the smaller volumes near the surface below offers the advantage of not hindering passage at ground level, whether for automobile traffic, a sidewalk, passageways in shopping centers, or an apartment interior. Having always lived in a city, I know that passageways should be as broad as possible in order to be able to walk about freely. So I tend to consider public parks, inscribed into a level area on the ground, as areas that compete with our means of circulation, also horizontal. The fact that we walk upright on two feet does not free us from horizontal movement but it does offer us the advantage of being able to dialog openly with the vertical world. Wandering in a public park comes from the desire to escape the urban atmosphere for a certain amount of time, while suddenly coming upon a vertical garden on some street angle encourages us to enter a world of imagination.

The juxtaposition of species within each vertical garden is obviously the essential element that influences how the piece is viewed globally. But the assemblage of living individuals must reflect an understanding of the evolution of each one of them over different periods of time. A garden should be perceived as a living and lush entity a few weeks after installation, but it should also evolve and recreate these first sensations after a few months, a few years, even decades later (a little less than three decades for my earliest vertical gardens).

And so I arrange side by side plant species that grow at more or less the same speed in order to avoid problems of competition and crown domination. In the case of a high vertical garden in the open air, I select for the uppermost areas species that are able to withstand strong winds, big differences in temperature, and the drying out of the irrigation cloth between two sessions of watering.

For vertical gardens on internal walls I envisage three zones, using tropical species alone: at the top I place large hemi-epiphyte species such as *Ficus*, *Schefflera*, *Clusia*, and *Philodendron* of the subgenus *Meconostigma*; in the middle section epiphytes from the trunks and major branches of trees (*Medinilla*, *Anthurium*, *Philodendron*, *Aeschynanthus*, *Rhipsalis*, *Asplenium*, *Drynaria*, *Nephrolepis*, etc.), and, toward the bottom, small saxicolous species from understory rocks or the banks of forest streams (*Pilea*, *Elatostema*, *Fittonia*, *Episcia*, *Begonia*, *Spathiphyllum*, *Aglaonema*, *Chamaedorea*, *Adiantum*, *Anthurium*). For open-air vertical gardens in temperate regions, I tend to prefer recreating a transect starting with plants from the summit of an exposed cliff (conifers, *Cotoneaster*, *Buddleja*, *Berberis*, *Abelia*); then, lower down, plants from rocky slopes and screes (*Lonicera*, *Hydrangea*, *Deutzia*, *Bergenia*, *Corydalis*, *Sedum*, *Carex*, etc.), and, near the bottom, plants from the understory or growing in the vicinity of streams (including ferns, *Heuchera*, *Tiarella*, *Saxifraga*, *Pilea*, *Boehemeria*, *Soleirolia*, *Epimedium*, *Luzula*, and of course *Iris japonica*). The creative ele-

In the summer of 2007 at the Musée du Quai Branly in Paris, after three years of growth, certain shrubs had to be pruned in order to prevent any chance of them falling on passers-by. But in fact, even shrubs taller than 20 feet (6 m), like the ones in Chaumont-sur-Loire, remain stable because of their roots' radial growth in the felt.

ment lies in the ordering of plant species for a particular wall and in the way they are juxtaposed. Sometimes I imagine a dense rainforest in Gabon or Ecuador, a karstic landscape in Malaysia or Cuba, an understory in South Carolina or Japan, a garrigue in Corsica or California, damp gorges in Chile or Australia, the ruins of Angkor or the walls of our ancient churches, or some completely fresh image that preys on my mind. Quite often I arrange the species in curves or in slanting or near-vertical lines as a reminder of the natural world, where we often find a particular species colonizing the entire length of an oblique crack in a rock face. It happens that when a seed is lucky enough to germinate in a favorable site, the resulting plant tends to colonize the available substrate, starting a population that gradually spreads downward as subsequent seeds fall. In order to achieve a harmonious juxtaposition of the spaces occupied by the plants, I pay attention to the structural characteristics of each species – the way the stems branch, the pattern of their external root systems, the density of their foliage, the size, shape, texture, and blade color of their leaves and how they absorb and reflect light. Thus, the plants are arranged on the basis of their ecological, structural, and chromatic characteristics, giving each vertical garden its own distinctive identity, which changes with the passage of time.

Since a vertical garden is by its very nature a kind of collective living organism, it needs to be looked after. For example, care must of course be taken not to interrupt the irrigation system for several days, especially in midsummer, and to provide additional lighting – and to do this correctly – whenever it is needed. Maintenance is often limited to a few inspections each year, usually once every four months for outside walls and every two months for inside ones. Certain species need no intervention at all, especially those growing in rosette form, producting a new leaf while an older one withers. On the other hand, species with well-developed stems, such as shrubs, need to be lightly pruned once a year to prevent their branches from getting too long. The tips of shrub branches should not be allowed to extend more than two yards from the support to prevent the plant's center of gravity from straying too far from the supporting structure. Unwanted species ("weeds") are either absent altogether or few in number owing to the verticality of the structure and the density of planting – about thirty to thirty-five plants per square yard. Access from ground level is by ladder or light scaffolding for walls only a few yards high, but for those from 30 to 100 feet (10 to 30 m) high, a vehicle-mounted cradle is necessary. For very high walls or where access is difficult, maintenance is carried out from the top by roping down from a mobile platform, like window-cleaners working on high buildings.

Verical gardens are proof that concrete is not an obstacle to biodiversity; on the contrary, it provides a support permitting the growth and survival of numerous fragile plant species. Walls in cities can thus become botanical gardens in a fragmented form, each of them expressing one aspect of a particular region's flora. It should not be forgotten that most endemic species with a very limited distribution originate from undulating rocky terrain and many of them from vertical environments. Through a rational choice of plants that takes account of their growth processes so as to avoid competition, it is possible to use a large number of species to cover a small surface area, on a wall of 100 square yards (100 m^2) I plant about a hundred species and on one of 1,000 square yards (1,000 m^2) up to between three and five hundred. In this way I come close to the tropical forest environment, where surveys have revealed that a 1,000-square-yard (1,000-m^2) plot contains an average of two hundred and fifty to four hundred vascular plant species. Nowadays, at a time when over half of humanity lives in cities, we need to show that nature can find expression in our urban environment and that the perception of its untrammelled and exuberant vigor will sensitize all those who live in cities to the need to safeguard what remains of the world's natural environments.

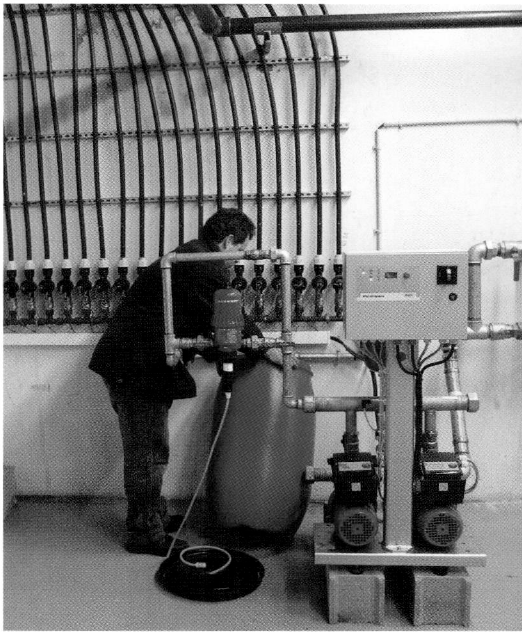

Sylvain tends the vertical garden in Avignon from a lift, accompanied by an operator. He then fills the reservoir with a nutrient solution, a task repeated about every month. From a simple irrigation control point all the tubes carry the water in turn to the different sections of the vertical garden.

Nicolas Lefranc is a professional tree pruner. He comes here to the Pershing Hall in Paris twice a year to trim the shrubs. From a horizontal steel bar attached at the top of the vertical garden, he rappels down using a long rope.

Works

INTERNATIONAL FESTIVAL OF THE GARDENS OF CHAUMONT-SUR-LOIRE, FRANCE, 1994 – PARC FLORAL, PARIS, 1994 – CONTEMPORARY ART CENTER, ALBI, FRANCE, 1997 – CARTIER FOUNDATION FOR CONTEMPORARY ART, PARIS, 1998 – VÉGÉTARIUM MUSEUM, LA GACILLY, FRANCE, 1998 – NAVE ITALIA AQUARIUM, GENOA, ITALY, 1998 – CULTURAL FORUM, LE BLANC-MESNIL, FRANCE, 1999 – HÔTEL DU DÉPARTEMENT DES HAUTS-DE-SEINE, 2005 – OLD BAKERY, FRANCE, 1999 – LES PASSAGES SHOPPING CENTER, BOULOGNE-BILLANCOURT, FRANCE, 2001 – HÔTEL PERSHING HALL, PARIS, 2001 – PALAIS DE LA DÉCOUVERTE, PARIS, 2001 – SHOPPING CENTER PROJECT, CRÉTEIL SOLEIL, FRANCE, 2001 – MARITHÉ AND FRANÇOIS GIRBAUD BOUTIQUES, PARIS, NEW YORK, OSAKA, 2002-2004 – NAUSICAA AQUARIUM, BOULOGNE-SUR-MER, FRANCE, 2003-2004 – A PRIVATE HOME, SEOUL, 2003 – FRENCH EMBASSY, NEW DELHI, 2003 – 21ST CENTURY MUSEUM OF CONTEMPORARY ART, KANAZAWA, JAPAN, 2004 – FAAP UNIVERSITY, SÃO PAULO, BRAZIL, 2004 – QUAI BRANLY MUSEUM, PARIS, 2004 – SOME PRIVATE HOMES 1996-2000 – IGUZZINI ILLUMINAZIONI SHOWROOM, PARIS, 2004 – KEN CLUB SPA, PARIS, 2005 – TERNES PARKING GARAGE, PARIS, 2005 – ICF BUILDING, BORDEAUX, FRANCE – VINET SQUARE, BORDEAUX, FRANCE, 2005-2007 – LES HALLES, AVIGNON, FRANCE, 2005 – CITÉ DE L'ESPACE, TOULOUSE, FRANCE, 2005 – CFDT FEDERATION, PARIS, 2005 – TERRACES, ITALY AND FRANCE, 2001-2007 – SIAM PARAGON SHOPPING CENTER, BANGKOK, 2005 – EMPORIUM SHOPPING CENTER, BANGKOK, 2005 – ESPLANADE SHOPPING CENTER, BANGKOK, 2007 – PARLIAMENT, BRUSSELS, 2006 – CAIXA FORUM MUSEUM, MADRID, 2006 – NICOLAS HULOT FOUNDATION, BOULOGNE-BILLANCOURT, FRANCE, 2006 – DELANNOY OFFICES, PARIS, 2007 – CLUB MED, PARIS, 2007 – BHV HOMME BOUTIQUE, PARIS, 2007 – PHYTO UNIVERSE CENTER, NEW YORK, 2006 – QUANTAS LOUNGES, SYDNEY, MELBOURNE, 2007 – CONCERT HALL, TAIPEI, 2007

Chaumont-sur-Loire was an all-round testing opportunity. In 1994 the world of temperate flora was relatively unfamiliar to me, unlike the tropical world. So I decided to test out many species, often going over budget, of course. But certain species, such as the superb fig tree, which became quite popular, were very common species.

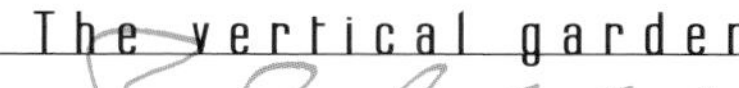

The moss gardens of Japan have always made the Western world dream. Mosses can colonize any humid surface that receives a minimum of light exposure. If you want to have moss develop on a horizontal surface like the forest floor, you must remove fallen leaves every day. That is precisely the morning ritual of the ladies at Kokedera, the famous moss garden in Kyoto. On a vertical garden wall, mosses and hepatics take strong hold because no fallen leaves cover them over.

International Festival of the Gardens of Chaumont-sur-Loire

Partial view of two of the vertical gardens, the *Agrostis stolonifera* waterfall, and a blossoming *Sedum spectabile*. This was probably the autumn of 1996.

The Vallon des Brumes (Misty Glen) was Jean-Paul Pigeat's idea. We hoped to recreate the ambiance of Far Eastern mountains. With the exception of arborescent ferns from Australia, all the species are Himalayan, Chinese, and Japanese. Several species were collected during official trips to Japan in 1995 and 1996. Among them you can spot some (non-urticant!) Urticaceae such as *Elatostema umbellatum* and the surprising *Boehmeria tricuspis*, with its trident leaves. As for the shrub at the top of the waterfall, it is a *Ficus erecta*, perfectly at home in our climate.

On the narrow side of one vertical garden, I wanted to create a permanent waterfall, but there are few temperate species confined to rocks which are continually being washed over with rather hard water. Walking along the banks of the Loire, not far from the Chateau de Chaumont, I noticed some grasses (*Agrostis stolonifera*) growing on shingle bars. I collected a few stems in order to place them on the waterfall and after only three months, they had covered the entire splash zone.

It was through these so-called ephemeral gardens that Jean-Paul Pigeat allowed us to pay homage to biodiversity. For anyone who knew a bit about plants, it was obvious that a garden designed to last only a summer could welcome temperate as well as tropical species. Every latitude was on display and we had a delightful time at it with my friend Éric Ossart, who was in charge of rounding up plants for each garden. I was thus able to educate the public about plant families that are often overlooked, such as Convolvulaceae, Solanaceae, and Urticaceae. In fact, it was after presenting my rather young collection of Convolvulaceae (the convolvulus and bindweed family) in 1996 that Bernard Viel, director of Green Spaces for the Hauts-de-Seine department at the time, offered to allow me to house and expand my collection in the arboretum greenhouses in the Vallée aux Loups park in Châtenay-Malabry. Chaumont proved to be a time for me to discover forest zones I had not yet visited, such as Chile's Valdivian forests in 1994 and the Kyushu forest of southern Japan in 1995, and even the forests of the southeastern United States in 1996. Jean-Paul Pigeat always knew how to introduce people likely to initiate an innovative project. Since the end of the 1980s (after I defended my thesis in science), it was largely thanks to funds from the Chaumont Festival, from the Comité International Interprofessionnel de l'Horticulture (CNIH), from the Radeau des Cimes missions, from television programs with Nicolas Hulot, and finally from the creation of vertical gardens around the world, that I was able to make field observations in new, hard-to-reach forest regions. By synthesizing my observations, I was able to develop new theories on the evolution of understory floras, tying together the global shapes of plants, the growth patterns, the types of fruits produced, the means of seed dispersal, the size and shape of the seed, and the seedling establishment micro-habitats. I was therefore able to offer new hypotheses to explain the relative richness specific to various regions. Chaumont and Jean-Paul allowed a large number of people to reach beyond their hopes and sometimes even beyond their abilities. It was marvelous.

International Festival of the Gardens of Chaumont-sur-Loire

After a dozen years, which included several cold winters and one long heat wave, this vertical garden, which purifies the water of the duck pond, remains luxuriant, and the public comes to sit on the benches.

Parc floral, Paris

During the opening of the Chaumont Festival, when I was presenting my vertical gardens for the first time to a larger public, Jacqueline Nebout was there. It was she who reigned over Paris's public parks for several years. It seems that Paris became much more verdant during that time, thanks to the creation of numerous gardens, parks, and squares. Upon seeing my gardens, Jacqueline Nebout told me, "I want one immediately for the Parc Floral." And two months later, that garden was complete. Its "vertical lagooning" system for water purification by the plants is quite interesting. The system was installed many years before those concepts became interesting to so many media and industries. In the Parc Floral, seeing that the space that I was offered sat along a large pool invaded by ducks and Florida tortoises, I felt that the green water might provide an excellent fertilizer. The water is filled with green unicellular algae that become trapped in the densely intricate fibers of the irrigation cloth. Once they are stuck in the fibers above the water level and subjected to alternating periods of hydration and dehydration, the algae decompose into a microhumus that gradually releases mineral elements which can then be absorbed by the roots of the plants in that vertical garden. And, naturally, all of the nitrates released from fish, tortoise, and duck excrement are also absorbed by the plant roots or by the microorganisms associated with them. I decided not to add any nutritive solution during watering. That vertical garden has been thriving since 1994.

The winter of 1997 was very cold: in 50° F (−11° C) weather, Pascal Héni walked on the frozen lake. Despite the low temperatures, the vertical garden is still there, more than a decade after its installation.

Contemporary Art Center, Albi

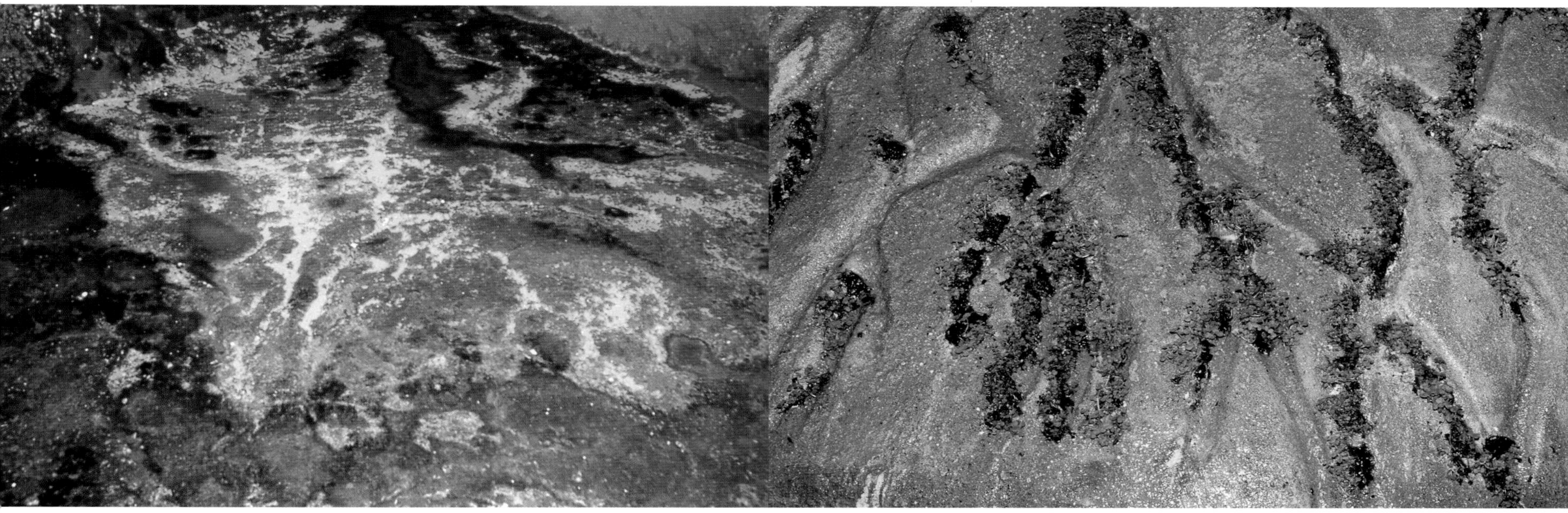

The iridescent green hepatic plant *Cyathodium foetidissimum* creates odd braided patterns along the rocky surface of a cave entrance in Gandhi National Park, north of Bollywood in Bombay. Ten years before that observation, I had created similar shapes on a resin-covered structure by installing *Chrysosplenium oppositifolium* in the artificial crevices. As for the 1/3-inch (1-cm) thick green blade, it is still thriving in the town square in Andillac.

The three people directly involved in the exhibit "In Situ In Visu" at the contemporary art center in Albi were the coordinator, Guy Tortosa, and the center's directors, Jacky-Ruth Meyer and her then associate, Jean-Claude Lattès. Among the artists invited to this exhibit in the summer of 1997, I recall Daniel Buren, Michel Blazy, Valérie Jouve, and Erik Samakh. Each one was allotted a space to develop. I was lucky to be given the Albi Mills along the Tarn, which I had known from earliest childhood since my father was from Montauban. Jacky-Ruth and Jean-Claude put themselves entirely at my disposal in order to see me succeed in this first contemporary art exhibit. Not wanting to repeat the work of Chaumont and the Parc Floral, I proposed two pieces: a green blade suspended from chains in the middle of the large vaulted hall, as well as an odd, kidney-shaped structure that recalled the wet rocks of the forest understory. The technical creation of these two pieces took place at Albi's school of fine arts. The "green blade" measured approximately 13 feet (4 m) high and 23 feet (7 m) long and consisted of a PVC pane held in a thin metal frame. From the side, the effect was surreal, since the plants seemed to come out of nowhere. When the exhibition closed, the green bridge was installed in the small wine-producing community of Andillac. I had covered the expanded polystyrene "boulder" in resin and then rough sand to produce a coarseness that would allow the roots to take hold. This was, therefore, my first attempt at a minimalist vertical garden: there was to be no irrigation cloth. The *Acorus gramineus* and *Chrysosplenium oppositifolium* were attached to the rough surface with a nontoxic glue and developed, irrigated by a pipe running along the crestline.

Cartier Foundation for Contemporary Art, Paris

Ten years after its installation, the vertical garden at the Cartier Foundation lets some species express all their potential, in particular the fig tree, the *Fatsia japonica*, the orange-flowered *Abutilon* and the *Pilea petiolaris*.

I was very warmly received at the Cartier Foundation. Hervé Chandès, along with his curators including Grazia and Hélène, invited me to participate in the exhibit "Etre Nature" (To Be Nature) alongside several other artists. A few years later, I asked for permission to adapt their title for the publication of my thesis, "Être plante à l'ombre des forêts tropicales" (Being a Plant in the Shade of Tropical Forests). During my first visit to the foundation, Hervé Chandès asked me, "Where on the building would you like to work?" I considered several sites, notably the immense pillars outlining the perimeter and the glass wall above the entryway. Covering the pillars was too complex for a temporary exhibit, so we stuck to the idea of a double panel for the glass pane above the entryway, covering the exterior with temperate plants and the interior with tropical plants. Jean Nouvel extended us permission to work on the building. It was then primarily with Hélène Kelmaechter, who quickly became a friend, that we undertook our project on these two surfaces. I was tired of reading, even from the hand of eminent colleagues, that biological diversity (the term *biodiversity* was not yet popular in 1998) was only important in the tropics and that the temperate zones were lacking in that respect. I decided to stir things up a bit by installing a wealth of luxuriant species on the outside wall and a relatively barren irrigation cloth on the interior, covered merely with modest *Anubias, Pogonatherum,* and Java moss. I particularly liked this interior piece, but I was one of few! The temperate plants outside were, however, very much admired. At the end of the exhibition, there was quite a debate: everyone who worked in the building strongly wished that the piece would stay in place. They prevailed, and ten years later, it is still there!

Virtual or real? The reflection of a cedar of Lebanon on the glass façade frames the vertical garden.

In nature, many species are rheophytes, meaning they grow in places that are permanently or intermittently subjected to strong currents, such as boulders jutting out of streams. Few tropical rheophytes are cultivated, but several ferns can be seen now and then, such as *Bolbitis heudelotii* and *Microsorum pteropus*, or even various species of *Anubias*, such as this *Anubias lanceolata*, native to West Africa.

Végétarium Museum, La Gacilly

My adventure with Jacques Rocher began about twelve years ago, when I installed a small vertical garden in the Yves Rocher boutique on the Rue des Tuileries in Paris. Several others followed. But the most interesting work came with the installation of the Végétarium in La Gacilly, a museum dedicated solely to plants. Parallel to numerous discussions about the museum's makeup and scenic decoration, Jacques offered to have me create a vertical garden that could express the biodiversity of tropical rainforests and the fragility of those ecosystems. Our work was all the more fascinating because there was no natural light in that closed space and it was essential to find the right lamps to allow for photosynthesis. Many micro-environments were created – understory waterfalls, wet rocks, a forest stream, cliff sections, and, of course, trunks and branches carrying epiphyte species. It seems that this botanical palette is still thriving today and that the large *Ficus*, *Schefflera*, and *Clusia* epiphytes require regular pruning.

Nave Italia Aquarium, Genoa

In 1998, I created two installations for museums: the Vegetarium in La Gacilly and the Aquarium in Genoa, Italy. In Genoa, the "aquariology" and "scenography" aspects were carried out by Nausicaa, under the direction of my friend Philippe Valette. The public aquarium already existed but had to be transformed following the reconstruction of the whole port zone by the Genoese architect Renzo Piano. Madagascar took center stage in the main hall of the aquarium and the fake boulders created by the Atelier Artistique du Béton in colored cement are reminiscent of *tsingis*, karstic structures eroded into jagged needles. The vertical garden was meant to show the broader biodiversity of tropical forests, and families – particularly rich in epiphytes and saxicoles, such as Araceae, Bromeliaceae, Gesneriaceae, Moraceae, and numerous other ferns, were well represented.

No biological break between interior and exterior: the 26-foot (8-m) circular glass allows a view of tropical plants from the courtyard and spring flowers from the offices.

Cultural forum, Le Blanc-Mesnil

Dominique Gaessler, an old acquaintance from university, was one of the two coordinators for this contemporary art exhibit, "Le temps déborde" (Time Spills Over) at the Cultural Forum. He contacted me and gave me a tour so that I could suggest a site for an installation. There in the Paris suburbs I wanted to avoid placing a barrier between the public and the installation. I was told that the piece would be vandalized or "tagged" (a slang term for marking one's insignia in graffiti), but I replied that installing a living entity in a natural and surprising way would surely be respected. And that was indeed the case: no plant has ever been uprooted or damaged despite the fact that the esplanade is used as a playing field. I was still obsessed by the idea of an interior-exterior continuum, and, fascinated by the glass measuring 26 feet (8 m) in diameter, I also offered to cover the interior of this 39-foot-(12-m)-square wall. The tropical-temperate juxtaposition here, which thereby guaranteed the inside-outside continuity, was meant to be perennial and I was assured that nothing would be destroyed at the end of the exhibition. It still stands, nearly ten years later.

After installing *Hoya linearis* many times in my gardens, I finally discovered it growing along sloping branches in Darjeeling and Sikkim, dangling in long supple strands, as they do here inside the Cultural Forum.

Hôtel du département des Hauts-de-Seine, Nanterre

Bernard Viel is the kind of faithful person who stays with you over the years. I think the first time we met was in Chaumont in 1994, in the company of Jean-Paul Pigeat. At the time, he was director of the public parks in the Hauts-de-Seine department, a region that has always been quite active in that area. When Bernard Viel invited me to participate, I was delighted. I had lived in the department for about thirty years, in Suresnes, and been to high school in Saint-Cloud. The commune selected for my project was Issy-les-Moulineaux, where I was born in the Clinique des Fleurs! The project was quite interesting and aimed to cover the gabled wall of a former industrial building on the Île Saint-Germain, a vast bakery that had lain abandoned since the turn of the century. Completed in 1999, that particular vertical garden thrived for several years before being torn down so the building could be restructured into a museum, a project that never came to fruition. A few years later, in 2005, Bernard invited me to adorn a tall concrete structure jutting from one of the façades of the huge hôtel du département in Nanterre. The project interested me for a couple of reasons: on the one hand, the structure was hideous; on the other, it was inscribed in a rather frigid urban framework. Nicolas Sarkozy was working there at the time. The public parks staff, whom I had known since working on the former bakery, were active participants in this project, along with Bruno Hyvernaud, to set up the the structure, and Sylvain Bidaut, to install the plants.

The old bakery

Les Passages Shopping Center, Boulogne-Billancourt

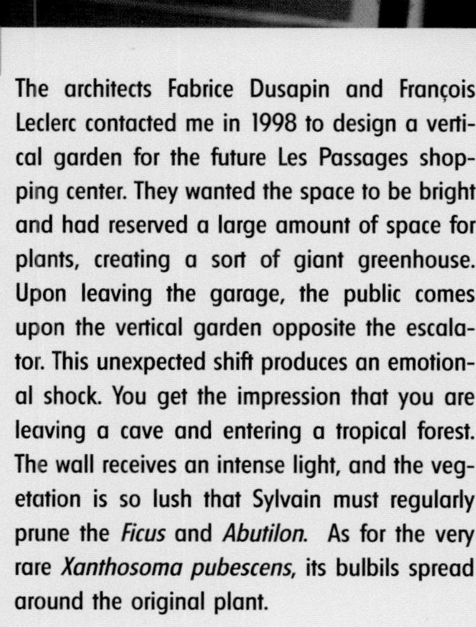

The architects Fabrice Dusapin and François Leclerc contacted me in 1998 to design a vertical garden for the future Les Passages shopping center. They wanted the space to be bright and had reserved a large amount of space for plants, creating a sort of giant greenhouse. Upon leaving the garage, the public comes upon the vertical garden opposite the escalator. This unexpected shift produces an emotional shock. You get the impression that you are leaving a cave and entering a tropical forest. The wall receives an intense light, and the vegetation is so lush that Sylvain must regularly prune the *Ficus* and *Abutilon*. As for the very rare *Xanthosoma pubescens*, its bulbils spread around the original plant.

Hôtel Pershing Hall, Paris

Life provides us with vital encounters: Andrée Putman was one of these. She arrived at my house one noontime – it must have been in 1997 – with our friends Éric Ossart and Arnaud Maurières, carrying baskets of oysters. Pascal and I didn't know who Andrée Putman was but we were fascinated with her gentleness, her curiosity, and her humor. She was wearing a wonderful chain-mail bracelet that had to have belonged to Rudolph Valentino. And her voice reminded me so much of Zarah Leander that I had no choice but to like her. When she left, after having looked at all the vertical gardens in our home, we still knew nothing about what she did. Then Éric told us simply, "She's the most influential interior architect." At the time I was far from that world because my creations had been mostly for parks and museums. The contemporary art world had just started becoming interested in my work, and the only architect who had approached me was Jean Nouvel. Soon afterward, we heard from Andrée: she was coming to see my friend Pascal Héni's recitals (he was not yet Pascal of Bollywood) in places as diverse as a barge and the Cartier Foundation. She invited me to participate with her in some television programs to discuss my work. At the end of 1999 or the beginning of 2000 she asked, "Patrick, can you save me?" I thought there was something important behind this appeal. She took me to visit the courtyard of a curious building near the Champs-Élysées, Pershing Hall, which had been the American headquarters in Paris following the First World War (it was named for General Pershing, who had led his troops to victory in France). It had since become a sort of annex for *Paris Match* magazine, and then eventually was abandoned. Two investors, Guy Assayag and Albert Lévy, had decided to transform the space into a hotel. They asked Andrée Putman to supervise the architectural changes and to create the interior architecture as well as all of the design elements.

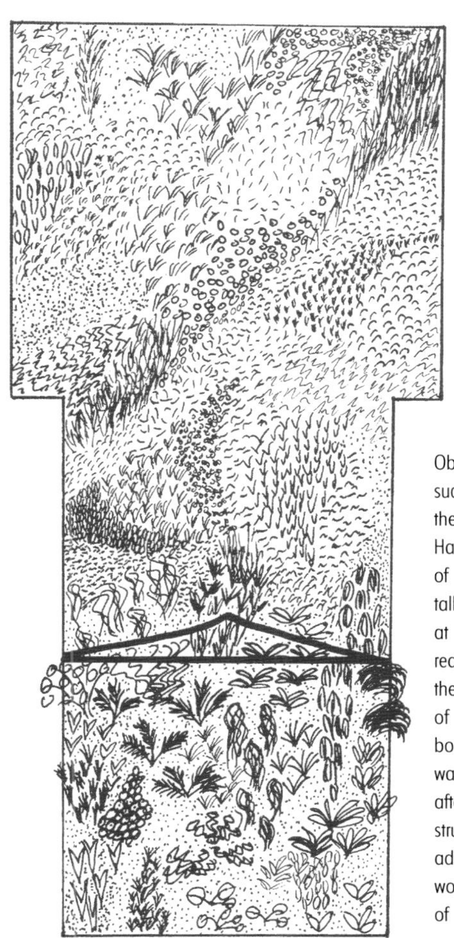

Obviously, Andrée Putman succeeded in persuading the owners of Pershing Hall to allow the creation of this vertical garden, the tallest one ever conceived at the time. In order to reassure them, I showed them a sketch of the range of various anticipated botanical landscapes. It was only a few months after that, with the construction of the wall quite advanced, that I actually worked out the sequences of plants for the layout.

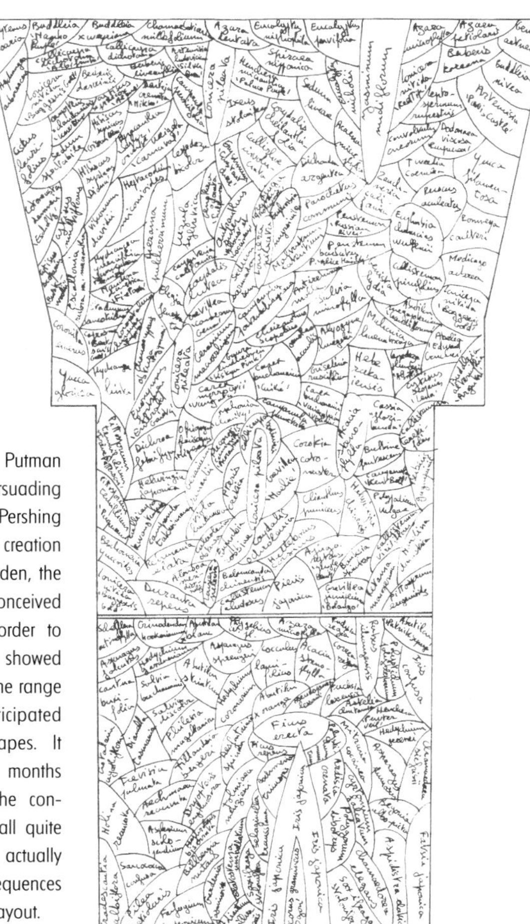

Just then Andrée realized that the whole building was centered on an immense open space 100 feet (30 m) high. One of its façades was a gabled wall that had not been restored in years. Creating a "boutique hotel" atmosphere around this unbearable sight was impossible. Andrée already knew what I would say when she called: of course I would be able to cover the wall (one of the tallest in Paris) with plants. It was the first time that I had been offered an intervention directly on the city itself. And the offer had not come from an architect or urban planner but, oddly enough, from an interior designer! A visionary architect. In less than a year, everything was ready for assembling the structure that would house the plants, and installation went off without a hitch. Along with the Emporium in Bangkok, carried out several years later, Pershing Hall's vertical garden remains my tallest creation. Now I have several new projects dealing with designing sequenced exterior cladding towers around the world.... Let us wait to see. But Pershing Hall will remain a symbol as the first great urban-botanical intervention in the world. Thank you, Andrée.

India is well represented in the lower section, which is protected by a sliding vellum during winter. The *Hedychium gardnerianum* blossom as if they were growing on their native hills while *Debregeasia edulis* display their long silver-backed leaves just as I discovered them on the cliffs of the Western Ghats.

Hôtel Pershing Hall, Paris

Palais de la découverte, Paris

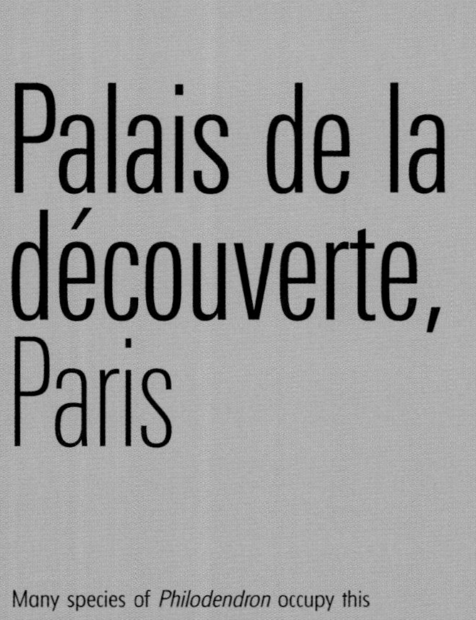

Many species of *Philodendron* occupy this section of the vertical garden.

The Palais de la Découverte was quite an adventure in 2001. My contact at the Palais was Patrick Buisson, with whom I have always freely exchanged ideas. The goal was to recreate a plant environment similar to that of French Guiana's social spiders that were to be housed in this room. These spiders construct vast webs among the plants growing along the forest edge, mostly shrubs, lianas, or low epiphytes. In order to recreate that particular habitat in a vertical garden, I gave precedence to lianescent and epiphyte species. I have been familiar with French Guiana's flora since my first trip in 1978 with Francis Hallé, while I was a postgraduate student at the University of Paris. After that I often went back, notably to the research center at the Nouragues Camp, which is run by the CNRS research laboratory I work in. I asked a student in French Guiana, Guillaume Fradet, whom I knew well since our stay in Nouragues in 1994, to collect plants for me, along with the necessary official authorizations. And so, *Philodendron fragrantissimum, P. pedatum, P. billietae, P. squamiferum* lie next to *Nephrolepis, Ficus, Clusia*, various *Anthurium*, Bromeliaceae, and Gesneriaceae. I am not sure whether the sublime *Markea coccinea* are still there but I thank Guillaume for his work. And the spiders are still around....

Several social spider (*Anelosimus eximius*) populations were installed on various shrubs behind a glass panel so that the public may observe them.

Shopping Center Projet, Créteil Soleil

For this open teepee extending from one level to the next through the opening, the outside surface of three cone sections was to be covered in plants.

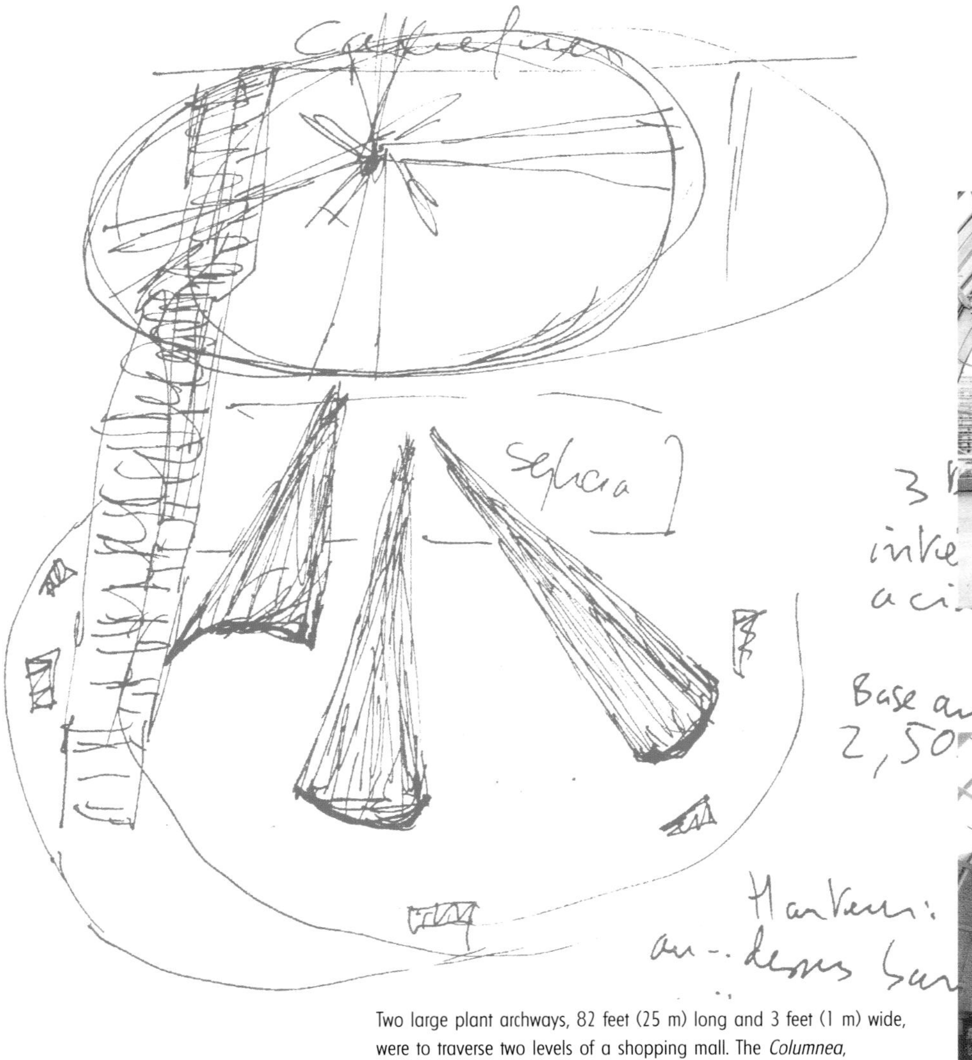

Two large plant archways, 82 feet (25 m) long and 3 feet (1 m) wide, were to traverse two levels of a shopping mall. The *Columnea, Aeschynanthus, Hoya,* and other *Rhipsalis* were to hang down 3 feet from each side of the arch while *Ficus diversifolia, Tradescantia spathacea, Medinilla magnifica,* and other ferns were to cover the toboggan-shaped surface.

The problem in shopping malls remains the same: what to do with these 3- to 6-foot (1- to 2-m) concrete strips separating each level around the central open spaces?

No, we are not yet at the Siam Paragon or the Bangkok Emporium. This is a virtual sketch for the Créteil Soleil project five years earlier. All these years later, I sometimes visit this space, still devoid of plant life in three dimensions.

In 2001 I was invited by SEGECE to redesign the plant layouts within the Créteil Soleil shopping mall. I found this amusing because I lived in the community, so I accepted, and participated in a sort of competition. Visiting every area, I wanted to come up with a different idea for each of them. I proposed about twenty designs. Some were structurally quite daring yet perfectly feasible. I made a rough sketch for each structure and Vincent Lagrue (who was an architecture student in Blois at the time) drew the final designs. It was disappointing to see the commission go to landscape architects who proposed a well-made classical layout. But the long hours of conceiving this project were not in vain because the plant arches and liana canopy were predecessors not only to the garden ceiling that I exhibited in 2006 at the Espace EDF Electra but also to an impending project in Rio de Janeiro. The suspended windscreens came to fruition four years later in Bangkok. As for the green sail, in the summer of 2007 it became the Green Vortex for Savannah College's contemporary art exhibit at Lacoste. And I am confident that the other pieces that I proposed, such as the open teepee, the double spiral, and the suspended pool, will be realized sooner or later, in one form or another.

Paris

What transparencies this place offers: shoes float among the plants, *Nolina* crawl toward the glass-sided elevator, *Aglaonema* deal effortlessly with passers-by, and under the open staircase, *Adiantum* occupy an area that evokes the limestone cliffs they came from.

New York

We created this green blade in New York, in the heart of Soho. Contrary to all of our expectations, it was much more difficult to find a wide array of plant species in New York than in Paris. But everything went well in the end and I revisited this garden in June 2007: still a beauty!

Marithé and François Girbaud Boutiques

This "Girbaud adventure" was a beautiful one. Marithé and François have always been fascinated by nature and by manipulating textiles to evoke natural wear while guaranteeing their longevity. If I remember correctly, it was Patrick Norguet, with whom I had already presented a piece for Van Cleef & Arpels, who introduced me to François Girbaud and Kristian Gavoille for this project for the large new boutique in the Rue du Cherche-Midi in Paris. Kristian proposed the location of the vertical gardens and it was up to me to accomplish the stimulating task of selecting the best species for each of the micro-spaces distributed along the four floors. We obviously needed to keep visitors (the potential boutique clients) interested, so I chose species that were markedly different for each floor. On the lower level, in order to evoke the atmosphere of a cave entrance, I used *Adiantum*, while at the top, in front of the windows, I installed *Abutilon*. After this, without a break, came the installations in New York and Osaka.

Osaka

What a pleasure it was to be able to work in Japan with unexpected species such as *Anthurium warocqueanum*. Kristian Gavoille perfectly utilized the coloring of leaves to design these strange mosaics on the accompanying walls.

Nausicaa Aquarium, Boulogne-sur-Mer

Thirty-five years after two adolescents steeped in the world of tropical fish formed a close friendship, it was quite a reunion: Philippe Valette had pursued studies in aquariology and became the director at Nausicaa, while I had undertaken research in tropical botany at the CNRS. Philippe got back in contact with me and, along with interior designers Geneviève Noirot and Christian Le Conte, we contemplated a makeover that would evoke tropical habitats for the Aquarium in Boulogne-sur-Mer. Upon seeing the imposing ventilation ducts jutting out over the tropical lagoon, I realized that they could be made to look like tree branches covered in epiphytes. I also proposed a curved green blade above the main pool, but the budgetary limitations did not allow for it. As for the concrete structures resembling karst reliefs, after three years of plant growth, they now resemble rocks from Khao Sok in southern Thailand with *Aeschynanthus, Cissus,* and *Nephrolepis* streaming down them. The *Philodendron, Rhoeo,* and *Columnea* are reminiscent of America, while the *Setcreasea, Zamioculcas,* and *Streptocarpus* take us into tropical Africa. The space is meant to evoke coastal cliffs along any of the tropical continents. A year later, we created the columnar gardens for the "Sale temps sur la Planète" (Bad Weather on the Planet) exhibition, and then a new space dedicated to caimans that I enclosed in a cylindrical vertical garden topped with a canopy of vines. My adventures with Philippe continue….

It's unfortunate that this green blade encroaching on a lagoon did not come to fruition. But that will be for another time. As for the concrete surfaces of the lagoon covered in algae, I kept them alive merely with an intermittent trickle of water, as on the vertical gardens. The substrate allowed for the germination of fern spores, notably *Adiantum*.

The columnar gardens of the "Sale temps sur la Planète" exhibition evoke the trunks of large trees covered in epiphytes in the world's remaining primary tropical forests.

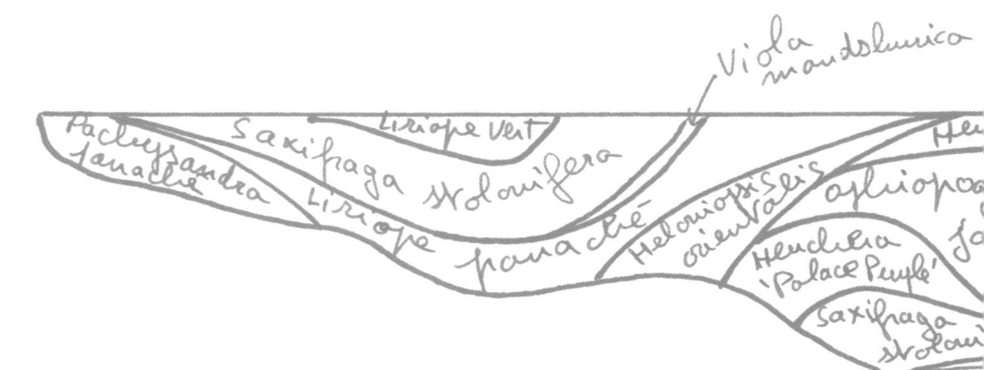

Private home,
Seoul

While I was discussing the Quai Branly museum with him, Jean Nouvel told me about his projects for a wonderful house in Seoul, where mineral and plant elements were to enhance each other. Since the amplitude of the broad curves of the granite were a few yards in length, I decided to create green sequences on the same scale. Unlike most of my creations where each species is allocated spaces about one yard long, here the *Liriope, Saxifraga, Heloniopsis, Mukdenia,* and *Euonymus* extend sometimes over 16 feet (5 m).

My realisation of the columnar gardens for the French Embassy is closely linked with Pascal of Bollywood's adventure. On Christmas Eve 2002 singer Pascal Héni and I met Jérôme Neutres in a Pondicherry hotel that had been transformed into an artists' residence by the owner, Raj de Condappa. Jérôme was the Embassy's cultural attaché and he asked Pascal, who was there to record some songs in Madras, to represent France for an official show during the next Indo-European summit in New Delhi. Rather than present a performance based on the French cultural heritage, the idea was to offer a recital with songs from Indian film heritage sung by a Frenchman, whose voice would obviously differ from that of an Indian singer. Pascal was quite a hit, as he was in numerous subsequent performances throughout India (he became known as Pascal of Bollywood). As this was unfolding, Ambassador Dominique Girard, who was familiar with my work, asked me to visit the Embassy's gardens, with the idea that a few of the surrounding walls could be used. After touring the imposing building designed by Paul Chémétoff in 1985, along with the gardens, I told Dominique Girard, "Mr. Ambassador, your Mughal-inspired gardens are certainly still growing but I don't see how I could intervene without somehow betraying the original concept. What's more, as you are aware, working with gardens in not my primary interest. However, when I crossed the main banquet hall within the Embassy, I saw that the four immense pillars holding up the building are sadly barren. They would come to life if they were covered in plants." The ambassador was enthusiastic, and I returned several months later as an artist-in-residence to work on installing the plants. The choice of species was rather limited since traditional Mughal gardens are mostly characterized by their structure and pathways, not by their plant diversity. Furthermore, Delhi's climate (cold in the winter and very hot in the summer) is not very favorable to growing tropical plants indoors – most plants are imported from the Bangalore area (which is not merely the Silicon Valley of India!). Installation of the plants, under Sylvain's direction as usual, went quite smoothly since the Indian workers understood the principle quite quickly. The columns were inaugurated in February 2004 by then-Minister of Foreign Affairs Dominique de Villepin, who had himself been French ambassador to India. Rather than ending quickly, receptions at the embassy now last so long that you need to invite guests to leave. The feeling of nature is even stronger since the Bombay bengalis (waxbills) bought from the Old Delhi market fly across the room from pillar to pillar, their song resonating in the enclosed space.

French Embassy, New Delhi

After three years, the plants growing perfectly and the *Schefflera*, along with several species of *Ficus*, were slowly creating a canopy above the *Nephrolepis* and *Philodendron*, while the *Pilea*, *Chamaedorea*, and *Spathiphyllum* flourish in the more shadowy sections at the base.

21st Century Museum of Contemporary Art, Kanazawa

I am honored to be among the eight permanent artists in this prestigious contemporary art museum, next to James Turrel and Anish Kapoor. Hervé Chandès, the director of the Cartier Foundation, told me that his friend Yuko Hasegawa, the curator of this museum-to-be, was very interested in my piece at the Foundation, and she was hoping I could design another for the museum in Kanazawa. Among my previous installations, the green blade of Albi held her attention. I proposed other, more audacious pieces, such as a vortex, but that seemed less well adapted to the site. I then went to Kanazawa to work out something new that would refer to the green blade. After an on-site discussion with architects Kazuyo Sejima and Ryue Nishikawa, it seemed that the green blade could be traversed by a glass tunnel and display one lit side and one shaded side. Already a little familiar with the flora of the region, thanks to a trip I had taken with Jean-Paul Pigeat a few years before, I decided to botanically contrast the two sides of the bridge. The shaded side would be dedicated to the local flora, while the brighter side would house species traditionally cultivated in the gardens of the area. On that first trip I wandered in the mountains overlooking the city (which were full of bears; several accidents had occurred at the end of the summer 2005, when a drought reduced the usual fruit production that the bears depend upon, and they took to the nearby villages). From the steep embankments I harvested samples of various species along the route, so that they could be cultivated over the next year. The Urticaceae were abundant, especially *Boehmeria tricuspis* and *Elatostema umbellatum.* Among other species I chose *Chloranthus serratus,* which belongs to a primitive family that I had studied in depth, *Carex nachiana,* with its plume of linear leaves reaching up to 3 feet (1 m) in length, *Epimedium sempervirens, Mitchella undulata, Ophiorrhiza japonica,* as well as some superb ferns such as *Arachniodes standishii* and *Coniogramme japonica.* All of the plants were cultivated and multiplied over one year, to be planted in the vertical garden at the beginning of summer 2004. The shady side resembled a fragment of mountain cliffside that a giant had cut away with a scalpel to place in the center of the museum. During the opening a few months later, visitors were fascinated by these plants, which seemed unfamiliar to them, and I explained that they grew on the boulders and mountain slopes an hour's walk from the museum! I needed to find a name for this piece and I dubbed it "Green Bridge," alluding to the bridge that must always connect nature to the city.

FAAP University, Saõ Paulo

It was Dominique Besse, a colleague from the CNRS working at the National Museum of Natural History, who contacted me with an invitation to participate in an exhibition she was to coordinate on the current and past biodiversity of the Chapada do Araripe hills, to be held at the FAAP University in Saõ Paolo. During my first visit we went to that area, and I immediately understood the biological interest in this small forest block isolated in the *caatinga* zone. It is the only patch of high moist forest between Amazonia and the Atlantic Forest (Mata Atlantica). Today it is an important biological forest refuge in the midst of drier vegetation zones, which explains the presence of different species of *Begonia, Philodendron, Piper, Psychotria,* and *Columnea.* I even found on wet shaded rock the iridescent *Cyathodium foetidissimum,* which seems to never have been noted in that area before. Due to a sedimentation process, highly favorable to fossilization, with a cycle of long, intermittent periods, this region is likely the richest in South America, particularly for the Aptian and Albian periods of the Cretaceous. There are a number of surprising plant fossils belonging to groups related to the first flowering plants that are currently under study. I spoke to Dominique about participating in the exhibition in two ways: on the one hand, by evoking this rediscovered record of the past biodiversity in the plant fossils; and on the other, by presenting the current biodiversity of the Brazilian rainforest. In terms of the fossil biodiversity theme, I decided to present a double spiral through which the public would be able to walk; this was obviously meant to recall the double helix of DNA that is the basis for the living world. The fossils in the Chapada do Araripe region stretch from the Devonian to the beginning of the Tertiary Era, so I decided to include each of the diverse plant groups representing these different epochs, for which there remain some currently living descendants. As visitors entered the double spiral of vertical gardens, they would discover *Psilotum,* then *Lycopodium* and *Selaginella,* then different groups of ferns, before coming upon Cycadales (*Zamia*), then Conifers such as *Podocarpus,* and finally the first groups of flowering plants, with current representatives such as Anonaceae (*Anona*), Chloranthaceae (*Hedyosmum*), and Piperaceae (*Piper* and *Peperomia*). In order to evoke the more recent periods of the Quaternary Era, I decided to create a labyrinth of suspended plant-covered panels punctuated with openings, reminiscent of cave dwellings along the cliffs of the Chapada used by its earliest inhabitants, from whom we find paintings and artifacts. I asked Jean-Bernard Robillard to arrange these plant panels and create a nice rhythm to these openings, a task he accomplished quite adeptly. As for the plants for this second section devoted to the more recent periods, it was easy enough to go to the local nurseries and find samples of the epiphytes and saxicoles that were native to the dense South American forest, most notably among the Bromeliaceae, Araceae, Cactaceae, Gesneriaceae, Urticaceae, and Piperaceae. And so past and present biodiversities were presented side by side.

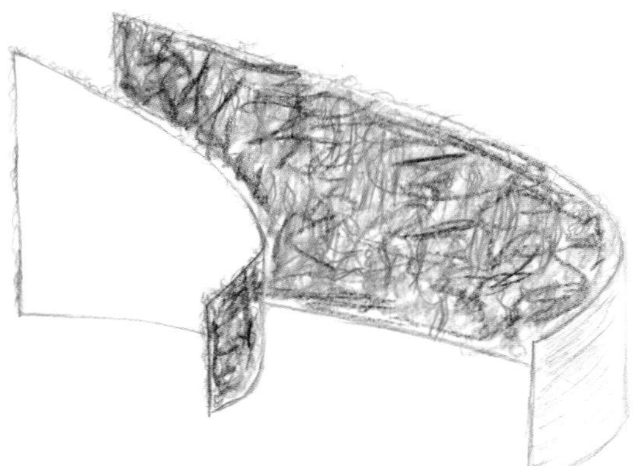

From the Spirals of the Cretaceous in one space to the Screens of the Quaternary at the other end of the exhibition, the plant world symbolized present life, and the incredible range of plant and animal fossils came back to life.

Passers-by are allowed to touch the plants, and that's fine. I had to argue against putting up any sort of barrier between the vertical garden and the public. I knew from previous installations in other places with a lot of visitors that most people are respectful of unusual creations that stir their emotions. Of course, a few fragments of *Helxine* are sometimes removed, but that is no problem since it grows back within a few weeks.

Quai Branly Museum, Paris

Perhaps the most representative, the vertical garden at the Quai Branly museum was not part of the original project. If I remember correctly, originally the façade of the administrative and research building was to be covered in overlapping metallic structures reminiscent of ivy. When Jean Nouvel asked me if it was possible to transform it into a vertical garden surrounding the immense windows, I told him of course that it would be no problem. And so Françoise Raynaud, who was in charge of the project during the planning phases, was given the task of modifying the call for bids on the façade and undertaking a survey in the neighborhood. At first it seemed that the people who lived in these Haussmann-era apartment buildings in the seventh arrondissement were not particularly enthusiastic, but little by little, they came to accept it. Today, they are the vertical garden's fiercest defenders. The setting up took place about three years later and the new project director, Isabelle Guillauic, coordinated the discussions with the builders and garden workers. Part of the problem was that we had to work with the façade builders for the structure itself and with the garden workers for the actual planting, all on a very limited budget. The metal framework had to be simplified, along with the waterproofing joints and the gutters for collecting water, the cause of a few untimely overflows, which nonetheless do not impede the growth of the plants.

Since Jean Nouvel wasn't happy with the imposed curved top line, he asked if it would be possible to add in some thicker, taller shrubbery there to soften the curve. That was his sole request. The façade measures approximately 13,000 square feet (1,200 m^2), with 8,600 square feet (800 m^2) covered by the vertical garden. I chose a range of species from the world's main temperate zones, essentially from the northern hemisphere (North America, Europe, the Himalayas, China, Japan). A few of the species were collected in Korea and Japan, such as *Elatostema umbellatum*, *Pilea petiolaris*, and *Ixeris stolonifera*. I also incorporated a few species from the southern hemisphere's temperate zones, such as *Berberis darwinii* and *B. linearifolia* from Chile and *Phygelius capensis* from South Africa. It was obviously impossible to include tropical species in the Paris outdoors, on a façade with northern exposure swept by air currents from the Seine. Yet I insisted that the biodiversity represented in this vertical garden echo the cultural diversity of artists the world over, whose works were on exhibit within that very museum. In the same spirit I selected about fifty photos that I had taken around the world and created a type of fresco 656 feet (200 m) long to surround the "boxes" jutting from the museum's façade. Each of these boxes corresponds to a region along the intertropical zone stretching through Africa, India, Southeast Asia, and Oceania. Selecting the photos from among my ten thousand slides was fascinating but involved more time than the plant installation for the garden itself! Everything came together in the summer of 2004, and a few of the offices ended up having smaller vertical gardens installed, which can be seen from outside through the windows. Reactions varied among those who worked in the offices: a few people feared being infected with exotic diseases, others hardly noticed, yet others took charge of the plants, pruning dead leaves and overgrown stems every morning. And the museum's director, Stéphane Martin, is still looking forward to adding tree frogs and lizards to his vertical garden!

Quai Branly Museum, Paris

Obviously I couldn't resist including *Iris japonica* at the Quai Branly, and just above them the *Pilea petiolaris* continue to develop year after year, partially covering over the *Helxine*. As for the *Heuchera*, between the natural species and the numerous new hybrids, the choice is extensive. Their hardiness is due to the fact that they are basically understory species that nevertheless tolerate intense exposure to direct light. But when I think of *Heuchera*, I always think of their leaves emerging intact from the melting snow in April, along the steep slopes in the shade of the giant sequoias in California.

Some private homes

A salon in Paris

When Marine Desproges-Gotteron called me twelve years ago, she simply said, "I found a marvelous spot in Paris, but save me. Just outside the living room, about three feet away, there are cement walls and I don't want a fresco." After visiting her place, I told her that there would be no problem in installing a vertical garden, though some supplementary light source would be necessary, given the cavelike feeling of the space. Everything came together rapidly, and Marine and Olivier came to number among my closest friends. You should see Olivier training the stolons of *Iris japonica* or planting *Begonia grandis* bulbils in new areas!

A private mansion

A new project with Andrée Putman, after Pershing Hall: in the narrow yet very deeply set courtyard of a mansion in Paris, an elevator was to be installed. Andrée and I decided that the elevator ride should evoke a climb through the forest, from the understory to the canopy. But because the natural light from above was insufficient compared to what is typical in the understory, additional lighting was supplied. This particular site's salient feature is the presence of three *Corydalis* species, namely *C. lutea*, *C. cheilanthifolia*, and *C. ochroleuca*, which all freely reproduce from seed.

A private swimming pool

I have had a wonderful friendship with Michèle Pilhan for more than ten years, thanks to this vertical garden I created to cover the wall and protect her indoor pool. There was only one problem that was never solved: Michèle cannot bear temperatures below 90° F (32° C), so it was necessary to choose species that could withstand those climatic conditions. But that is one part of this never-ending experiment that is so fascinating.

iGuzzini Illuminazioni showroom, Paris

Architect Pier Luigi Copat contacted me about creating a new showroom for the iGuzzini lighting company in Paris. The location is next to the contemporary art center "La Maison Rouge" (The Red House), and red was also the dominant color chosen for the showroom. This created an amusing confusion among visitors. I was strongly interested in the project because the situation was totally unprecedented: the first section of the vertical garden was to be in an entry corridor that would be exposed to the outside air temperature but received no light; the second section was to be installed inside under a glass ceiling. This was the opposite of what we normally encountered: a temperate space outside without light and a tropical space inside flooded with natural light. Of course, with iGuzzini, we had no problem solving lighting issues and the two vertical gardens separated by a sheet of glass continue to thrive, with a pool of fish (red, obviously!) swimming from one side to the other.

Ken club spa,
Paris

It was quite amusing to see Arthur and Frank-Elie Benzaken negotiate the copyright issues for this project. Arthur was so touching as the poor heir inviting billionaires into his club that I accepted his complaints ... and I don't regret it. My gardens have behaved very well over the years and I maintain an excellent relationship with these brothers, especially since they take very good care of my "baby," with the help of Sylvain, of course, who comes for control visits. When Arthur offered to have me intervene in this overly concrete area, it was merely a question of surrounding the solarium with vertical gardens. I told him that the whole space needed to blend into nature and that the stairway and pool needed to "float" among the plants. He accepted, and what a joy it is now to see, within this protected space, cascades of *Iris japonica*, *Iris confusa*, *Fuchsia regia*, *Pilea petiolaris*, and even an indeterminate *Pilea* collected from beside a Sikkim temple.

No difference between inside and outside. The ferns outside are of course *Cyrtomium* and *Polystichum* whereas those within are *Nephrolepis* and *Platycerium,* but what difference does it make? The cliff of leaves crosses the mirror.

Looking down on the garden from the upper deck of the parking garage is breathtaking: the plant species alternate up the 50-foot (15-m) column. Certain species, such as the *Zebrina* and *Epipremnum*, spread onto the concrete flooring of the last level.

Ternes parking garage, Paris

Here's to Edouard François, the fashionable French architect beloved of women and known for his desire to be innovative in the use of plants on buildings. Jean-Paul Pigeat invited Edouard and his then-associate, Duncan Lewis, to construct a very odd and interesting greenhouse in Chaumont made of transparent PVC on bamboo. This was one or two years after the success of my vertical gardens and Edouard was interested in working with me. A short time later, he created his "growing building" in Montpellier, but the plants did not grow as well as he had hoped. Despite this, the apartment building was stunning. Later, he was to rehabilitate the Ternes parking garage in Paris, and suggested bamboo in containers laid out horizontally on each level, as can be seen from the sketches of his project. He asked me which might be the best species to work with, and looking over the designs, I asked, "But why a horizontal layout that yet reinforces the parking levels, when there are broad open wells running along the elevators that could house botanical columns?" He was intrigued by the idea and we asked the contractor to modify the original plan, which he immediately agreed to do. The staged installation of the seven columns took place without a hitch, but secure access for upkeep, a subject of much discussion between the parking garage owners and the architect, was never agreed upon. That has been the situation for three years. Fortunately, wherever there are lamps still functioning to induce photosynthesis, the plants are growing marvelously, as recent photos show. Another enjoyable project with Edouard was to cover a chimney at La Défense, and I am sure we will meet again on new projects.

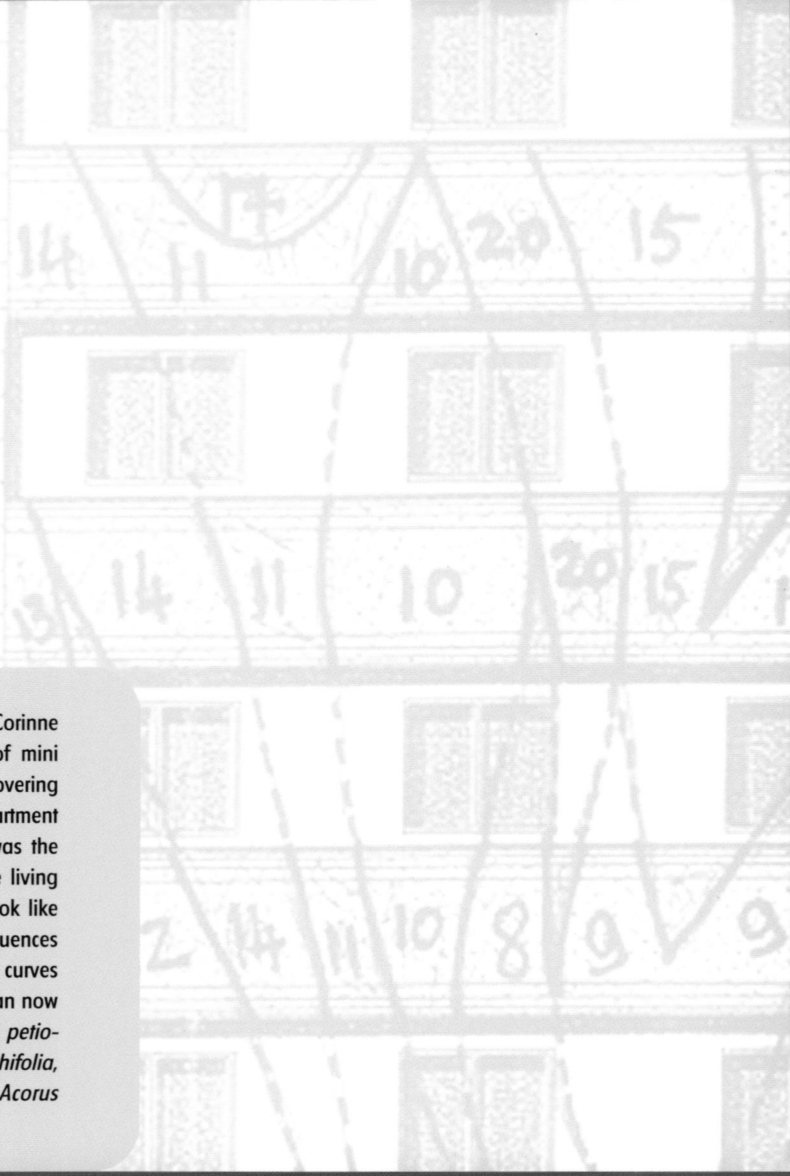

ICF Building, Bordeaux

Having seen my work at Vinet Square, architect Corinne Page proposed an amusing installation, a sort of mini Siam Paragon for outdoors. It was a matter of covering strips of concrete between the floors of an apartment building. I was even more interested because it was the first time that I would be working with a collective living space. In order for the four layered strips not to look like hanging plant containers, I worked out plant sequences stretching from one floor to the next, working along curves up the full height of the building. As a result, one can now see the long diagonals of *Iris japonica* and *Pilea petiolaris* (of course!), as well as *Corydalis cheilanthifolia, Phygelius capensis, Fuchsia magellanica, Acorus gramineus, Lonicera pileata*....

Vinet Square, Bordeaux

Michel Desvigne is one of the few landscape architects with whom I have worked, and did so with much pleasure. He was in charge of restructuring a small square situated in the heart of old Bordeaux, and he thought about bordering the space with a rather long vertical garden (about 325 feet [100 m]), comprising an alcove reminiscent of a cave. His plans seemed perfect, and I made only minor modifications. I met with Elisabeth Vigné, assistant to the mayor of Bordeaux on environmental issues, who was overseeing the project. Elisabeth, a delightful and combative person, saw that everything was completed on time. The public parks team for the city of Bordeaux truly brought efficient and gracious support to creating the infrastructure, and installing the vertical garden under these conditions was a pleasure. It was the first time that I was creating a vertical garden in a space dedicated to young children, and I kept several aspects in mind: foremost, the plants within their reach had to be totally safe (neither poisonous, spiny, nor stinging). I was also aware that children see circular shapes better than linear shapes and bright colors better than pastels. It was exhilarating to organize the plant layouts working within those parameters, and nearly three hundred species were planted in that garden.

Les Halles, Avignon

In creating the plant layout I was guided by the fact that the garden was almost entirely visible from Place Pie, from a distance of several dozen yards. Unlike other gardens that are viewed from within a few feet, where the scale adopted was that of a few inches, I decided here to work at the scale of about one yard. Certain species seem to be colonizing slanted cracks along a cliffside, spreading 10 to 16 feet (3 to 5 m) long. *Iris japonica* stretch over 65 feet (20 m) across the garden.

At a café terrace on Place Pie, Pascal (of Bollywood) and Sylvain Bidaut relax as the vertical garden begins its second growing season.

PLACE PIE

The Avignon market hall was hardly breathtaking, despite the fact that it is in one of the city's main squares. It was Marie-Josée Roig, the city's mayor, who got in contact with me after seeing my garden at the Quai Branly museum. She asked me to screen the canvas hiding the five-level parking garage on one side of the square. I told her that the idea seemed perfectly workable, but that it would be even better if the alcoves on either end could also be transformed into vertical gardens. You wouldn't then find yourself in front of a flat section of cliff but more in the midst of a rocky labyrinth reminiscent of the karst reliefs of the area. Madame Roig immediately agreed to these additions, and a few months later, the garden was planted. It was on that 6,500-square-foot (600-meter^2) surface that I planted the widest range of species, more than three hundred different species. We used many Mediterranenan species (*Cistus, Helianthemum, Dianthus, Salvia, Cytisus …*) as well as some dwarf conifers. I kept in mind that the wall faced north and would be exposed to the full mistral winds. Planted in the winter, for some time it resembled an odd purplish floor cloth dotted with small tufts of hay, but soon the irrigation cloth took on a greenish hue as the microflora grew, mostly blue-green and green algae, then mosses and hepatics took over as the plants themselves began producing small leaves in February.

AMERIQUE
AFRIQUE
Ficus lyrata

Cité de l'espace, Toulouse

The architect Véronique Kirchner was chosen to create the new Astralia site in the Cité de l'Espace in Toulouse; Olivier Ferracci was in charge of design. This space, which was also dubbed the Sixth Continent, focused on voyages in space, and it was interesting that, just before being swallowed by the imposing movie theater, the public was given a vision of nature from our earthly world. The large vertical garden swoops over a whole section of the entrance hall. Because the site has a pedagogical function, I decided in the end to present a global, equatorial view of the Earth, displaying in succession the tropical epiphytes and saxicolous flora from the three continents traversed by the equator. Surveying the garden from left to right, you see flora from South America, then Africa, and finally Asia. In order to separate the continents, I used *Nephrolepis exaltata*, a fern that lives throughout the entire intertropical zone. A few genera, such as *Ficus*, are also common to the three continents, but species vary from one continent to the next. To evoke the Americas, I chose several Bromeliaceae (*Billbergia, Aechmea, Cryptanthus . . .*) since that family is endemic to the Americas, but also a number of Araceae (*Philodendron, Anthurium*), Gesneriaceae (*Columnea, Nematanthus . . .*), Cactaceae (*Rhipsalis* and similar genera). In Africa, the range of epiphytes is narrower, but saxicolous plants are well represented. Besides several African species of *Ficus* (*F. lyrata, F. cyathistipula, F. natalensis*), I blended the sequences with *Streptocarpus, Saintpaulia, Zamioculcas, Clivia. . .* As for the Asia section, I had a broad selection to choose from of *Medinilla, Aeschyanthus, Hoya, Ficus,* and *Asplenium* for the upper sections, recalling the main branches of tall trees covered in epiphytes. The lower portions evoked understory boulders, with *Ludisia, Aglaonema,* and *Alocasia.*

Françoise Raynaud, with whom I had worked on creating the vertical garden at the Quai Branly museum, won the competition for creating the new CFDT headquarters in Paris with a plan for lining the entrance ramp to the parking garage with plants. In such an urban setting she decided to create fake rocks, asking me if it was possible to have them partially covered over in moss. Since she was familiar with my work, her proposal was obviously likely to receive a positive response from me. With Bruno Hyvernaud, who had already worked on the construction of so many vertical gardens, we discussed the best places from which to let water trickle down to ensure plant development directly on the concrete. I had already approached the Ateliers Artistiques du Béton, which was in charge of creating the boulders, about covering them with a non-toxic coating. I installed *Helxine, Adiantum,* and some hepatics along the irrigated interstices. Two years later, they had grown so well that I now hesitate to systematically install irrigation cloths on some of my gardens! In order to give more balance to the piece, I spoke with both Françoise and with Youssef Baccouch, who was financing the project and was always open to my suggestions, about partially covering the walls across from the boulders and installing rustproof steel cables above the car entrance so that climbing plants could grow into areas inaccessible to vertical gardens. All of that was approved, and now I have several projects that include lianas "escaping" from my vertical gardens.

On the fake concrete boulders slightly tinted green, mosslike plants such as some *Helxine* (green *Soleirolia soleirolii*, and the cultivar 'Aurea') and maidenhair ferns (*Adiantum* 'Fragantissimum') are growing along the vertical cracks that conduct water from the spigots at the top. You get the sense of being in a cave or among the glistening boulders of the understory.

CFDT Federation, Paris

Across from the mossy fake boulders, on the other side of the parking garage's entrance ramp, two vertical gardens climb toward a school's railings. The children thus enjoy blooming *Fuchsia*, while *Helxine* overflows on the concrete panes and in the gutter along the bottom.

Terraces, Italy and France

The terrace of Renata and Miguel Chevalier, the latter an artist who creates virtual plants with light sequences.

I always derive pleasure from installing pieces in private homes when the site inspires me or if I feel that a friendship might result from it. Of course, with larger projects becoming more frequent, private vertical gardens are becoming less common. This large patio at a superb home in old Lecce, in southern Italy, used to have a rather sad wall that was quite tall across from the entry and I immediately accepted the offer to transform it into a vertical garden, especially since the mild climate allowed me to include plants that were sensitive to cold, such as different species of *Impatiens, Begonia, Hemiboea, Debregeasia, Ficus,* and *Hedychium.* In the heart of Montmartre, Maren Sell (who had not yet become my editor) asked me to "do something" to block the view of the neighbors; I simply decided to use tall shrubs at the top of a vertical garden around the terrace and to create a sort of small recess for shade-loving plants and hiding the pumps. Just behind the Invalides in Paris, a new private vertical garden was created, and there again the neighbors could look directly down on the central patio; thanks to steel cables attached at the top of the vertical garden around the patio, I grew numerous species of climbing plants to create a kind of bower. Elsewhere, a few protected spots allowed me to incorporate some *Woodwardia, Nephrolepis, Abutilon…*

Siam Paragon Shopping Center, Bangkok

My work with the Boiffils, Jacqueline, Henri, and eventually their son Basile, was a fascinating and wonderful experience. At first, it was a bit strange: they were trying to get in contact with me and I didn't reply, then one day, my assistant Jean-Luc le Gouallec, on a trip to see relatives in Bangkok, told me about a project for a new shopping center in Bangkok, with my vertical gardens adorning the magnificent entryway, similar to what I had proposed a few years earlier for the renovations on the Créteil Soleil shopping center. It was through Supaluck, the future owner of the site, that I was put in contact with the Boiffils. Already familiar with my vertical gardens, the Boiffils integrated them perfectly into that space and I made no changes to the long, suspended bands evoking an old Italian-style theater; however, we worked together with Henri to outline the shapes and layout of the panels in the central fountain. Supaluck had been taken with the panels I created at FAAP University in Saõ Paolo and she basically wanted replicas. Everything was coming along smoothly, with some amusing steps in between, such as the financial negotiations with Supaluck, a remarkable businesswoman. I explained to her that the reason for accepting conditions below my usual request was simply because I was delighted to work in Bangkok, which I had loved since the age of nineteen, during my first adventure into tropical forests. Afterwards, everything came together remarkably well thanks to the immediate response of the local teams and the incredible diversity of plants available in Thailand.

ARMANI
HERMÈS

Siam Paragon Shopping Center,

Bangkok

I should mention that in Thailand it is mostly women who are the effective project leaders. My privileged contact for this project (as with the Emporium) was Siriluck and we spent some wonderful time together in the Bangkok nurseries as well as the Khao Yai forest. Siriluck was often quite worried because vertical gardens were novel in Thailand. I mostly chose my plants in the Chatuchak market at first. There are over five thousand different plants on display there every Wednesday and, to my knowledge, Bangkok has the greatest biodiversity in the world in terms of cultivated plants. There I discovered the impressive nursery near Ayutthaya, northwest of the city, the Tanowasri Fern Nursery, run by the Nagean family. Even in the world's most renowned botanical gardens, I don't think I've ever seen such a range of ferns and club mosses. Moreover, their *Rhipsalis* collection is astonishing. Since I wanted the plant strips (dubbed "Hanging Fences") to recall mighty epiphyte-covered branches of tropical forest trees, I opted for species likely to stream down over one or two yards (1 or 2 m). That's why I chose about fifteen species of *Rhipsalis,* alongside *Anthurium vittariifolium, Nephrolepis acutifolia, Aeschynanthus,* and various *Dischidia.*

In order to make a distinction between the Emporium and Siam Paragon, I decided to recreate the lush atmosphere of a tropical forest in the Emporium, since each column along the elevator reached the real proportions of a tree trunk in a tropical forest: 100 feet (30 m) high with a 3-foot (1-m) diameter. About fifty epiphyte species now adorn those "trunks." As for the panels immersed in water, they recall the karstic outcrops of Along Bay and are in some ways a precursor for my installation in the Espace EDF Electra.

Emporium Shopping Center, Bangkok

The first project I created in Bangkok with the Boiffils was in the rather chic Emporium shopping center, on Sukhumwit Road. They had designed the center ten years before and decided with the owner, Supaluck, to renovate it so that it would stand the comparison with Siam Paragon. When you are lucky enough to have the opportunity to work in a country discovering a new concept in urban planning, it seems that everything is possible. So when Jacqueline and Henri asked me to line both sides of the elevator shaft with plants over 100 feet (30 m) high, I of course accepted, but realized that the task was not simple. In fact, each strip is only 3 feet (1 m) wide and the Oriental restaurant is located just below, only a few inches removed from the plants. The irrigation system needed to be designed so that the water would flow over a narrow surface without dripping onto the clientele below. With Siriluck's help, all of the discussions with the people involved went smoothly and Sylvain led a very competent team in some rather acrobatic planting. Two years later, the *Philodendron goeldii* have become so full at 82 feet (25 m) high that they remind me of my first images of French Guiana in 1978 when I discovered some of them clinging to the tops of tree trunks on Kaw mountain.

Again with the Boiffils, for the Esplanade project. But this time it was more of a discussion with Basile, their architect son. In fact, it all began over dinner in Bangkok where we were discussing creating a new site with Nopporn in Sukhumwit; he told me that prior to that, he would like me to work quickly (meaning, within the coming three months!) on the new Esplanade shopping center designed by Basile in Ratchadapisek, across from the Thai Cultural Center. When I visited the site, which was quite advanced in construction, I felt that the only place I could work on was the façade: there were five lateral columns depressingly covered in metal, visible from all around. Covering the columns in plants was especially interesting to me since it would constitute my first outdoor vertical garden installation in a tropical zone, and I had dreamt of doing this for years. It all went well and I chose the species with Janewit in Chatuchak and in nurseries north of Bangkok. The rate of plant growth is surprising and it is necessary to keep an eye out so that the *Heterocentron*, for example, don't take over. But we were, after all, in conditions equivalent to that of a forest edge and the competition between species is higher there than in the understory. What a joy to see, depending on the amount of sunlight received, the *Medinilla, Pereskia,* and *Russelia* covered in blossoms, while the *Philodendron* 'Lemon Lime' and various *Ophiopogon* and *Episcia* become more and more exuberant!

Esplanade Shopping Center,
Bangkok

The pink irrigation cloth is installed on the PVC, and the irrigation tubes as well! Sylvain has already transferred the layout of plant species with chalk. Everything is ready for plant installation on this column; the other one was planted the night before. Everything moves quickly in Bangkok!

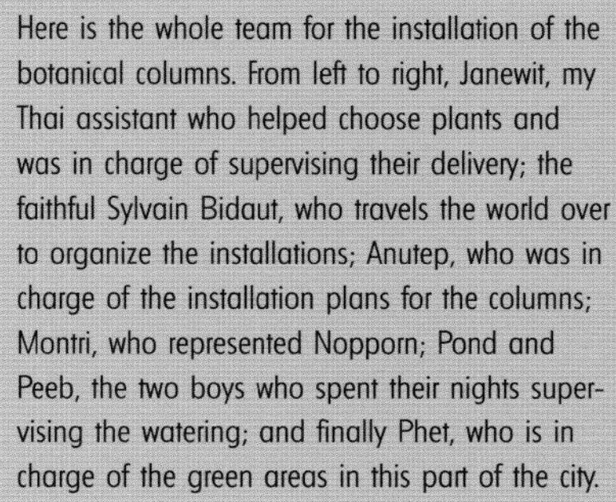

Here is the whole team for the installation of the botanical columns. From left to right, Janewit, my Thai assistant who helped choose plants and was in charge of supervising their delivery; the faithful Sylvain Bidaut, who travels the world over to organize the installations; Anutep, who was in charge of the installation plans for the columns; Montri, who represented Noppon; Pond and Peeb, the two boys who spent their nights supervising the watering; and finally Phet, who is in charge of the green areas in this part of the city.

Parliament, Brussels

Working with the architectural firm Art and Build along with landscape architect Christophe Spehar, we envisioned a project to cover the broad surfaces of the central courtyard with vertical gardens for the renovation of the Brussels Parliament building. It was once again a large-scale project, because the dimensions involved were quite large. If I remember correctly, the chimney that I covered with a vertical garden is around 100 feet (30 m) high. After several problems with temperamental irrigation systems, the plants have now thickened out and the diversity of species I have selected for each one of the variously oriented vertical gardens here is now becoming more apparent. In Europe outside France, Belgium was the first country to take interest in my work. I have always been warmly welcomed when designing my various projects there.

Caixa Forum Museum, Madrid

I went to Basel to meet Jacques Herzog and Pierre de Meuron to discuss several projects, but especially the future museum of contemporary art, Caixa Forum, on the Avenida Prado, across from the botanical gardens and the Prado Museum. The project pleased me immediately since it represented the largest blank wall I had yet to cover with a vertical garden. I had 6,458 square feet (600 m^2) at my disposal for my plant sequences, which allowed me to recreate some veritable natural settings. This vertical garden is also adjacent to a new square that is completely accessible to the public, who can reach up and touch the plants. I had to keep Madrid's climate in mind: scorching in summer and cool in winter. And so I chose nearly three hundred different species, many of which come from Mediterranean climates. On site, Carlos Gerhard and Valentine Laperche were extremely helpful in coordinating the various participants in this gigantic project. Everything went incredibly well, but there were delays in the work and the water was unfortunately cut off twice in high summer for several days. This created the obvious consequence: many plants dried out. Fortunately, quite a few of them revived, but we had to repair a section of the vertical garden. Now that the building has been completed, the lush plants blend perfectly into the surroundings, particularly with the reddish ochre of the chiseled cast-iron façade. I have other projects with Herzog and De Meuron, most notably on completely covering some buildings in Santa Cruz de Tenerife.

Nicolas Hulot Foundation, Boulogne-Billancourt

I have known Nicolas Hulot for more than twenty years, starting when he was on the radio after having been a photographer and a stuntman. He was among the first to invite me to talk about the scientific mission with the Canopy Raft in French Guiana in 1986. A little while later he invited me back to speak about my vertical gardens, which had not yet left the confines of my apartment except for the panels that I had installed for the green bridge at the Cité des Sciences et de l'Industrie de La Villette in Paris. Then his television program "Ushuaïa" began and in 1991 he asked me to film a piece on my research in Malaysia. I believe it remains the most extensive coverage to date about plant adaptation to the shaded conditions of the forest understory. Our filming adventures continued over the years: on Mount Ruwenzori, in eastern Africa, on the Venezuelan *tepuis,* along the high-altitude lakes of Bolivia, in the mangroves and mountains of New Guinea, as well as among the *Dracaena* and *Adenium* on the Socotra Island. For the last several years, I have also been a member of his foundation's Comité de Veille Ecologique (Committee on Ecological Supervision). The foundation is currently led by my friend Cécile Ostria, who wrote a thesis on the peat bogs of the Andes in our Tropical Botany laboratory at the University of Paris, under the direction of Professor Schnell. Nicolas is currently involved with environmental problems around the world. When he asked me to create a vertical garden in his foundation's new headquarters, I immediately accepted, considering it almost a necessity to showcase a few aspects of biodiversity in this particular place!

When you arrive at the top of the staircase, you face this vertical garden, a recreation of the gradient from canopy to understory in tropical forests, condensed to a 9-foot (3-m) height. At the top, hemi-epiphytes including *Schefflera, Ficus,* and *Clusia* crown the larger, erect epiphytes *Medinilla, Billbergia, Anthurium,* and *Asplenium*, under which hang *Nephrolepis, Rhipsalis, Columnea,* and *Aeschynanthus.* At the very bottom, *Chamaedorea, Spathiphyllum,* and *Aglaonema* flourish in an understory atmosphere.

Delannoy Offices, Paris

Catherine Delannoy was walking through the fourteenth arrondissement in Paris and stopped to daydream below the vertical garden that she spied through the curtains of a second-story loft. This was the interior vertical garden that I had created for Jean-Marc Dimanche. She tried to contact me but, as I was probably in the field in a tropical forest somewhere, I didn't get back to her. Quite determined, she succeeded in contacting Jean-Marc and ended up finding me. The new site for her agency was perfect for creating a vertical garden linking the different floors. The narrow gorge reminds me of the hidden glens of the backcountry near Nice.

Club Med, Paris

When Club Med moved a few yards away from the Champs-Elysées, they decided to create a space that evoked nature's diversity and the mellowness of their destinations. The interior designer François Hannebique asked me to reflect on how to organize vertical gardens to reflect the diversity of the sites that welcome their clients. I immediately thought of creating a succession of the three tropical continents America, Africa, and Asia. There was not a lot of height, so I created a broad ribbon crossing the intertropical zone. This green ribbon evoking the equator turned at right angles between the African and Asian zones. Perfectly lighted, this vertical garden always exhibited a surprisingly dynamic growth.

Most outdoor vertical gardens need maintenance three times a year: in the spring, in high summer, and at the end of the fall. This recent garden, installed in December 2006, received its first control visit by Sylvain Bidaut in August 2007, using a mechanical lift. There was little to do: simply prune the hearty *Buddleja* and *Weigela*, cut back a few *Sedum*, and untangle the *Pilea petiolaris* so that they would hang freely about the sign.

BHV Homme Boutique, Paris

When architect Frank Michigan asked me to work on the façade of a new BHV Homme storefront, in the heart of the Marais district in Paris, I was quite interested and the project received a favorable welcome, especially since Pascal Héni and I were already familiar with the people directing the Galeries Lafayette group. In fact, I only had to fit inside the area that Frank had left for us, since it was so perfectly defined. The only problem was the scheduled planting time, which had to take place in December for an opening that was to occur in early March. The plants would only have a short growing period before the opening so I decided to plant a wide array of species very close together. There are over a hundred species on approximately 1,300 square feet (120 m^2). A miracle occurred and each of the plants had filled out enough over the three winter months in 2007 (a very mild winter), and this vertical garden earned enthusiastic praise. In the following months, the plant diversity was such that the garden offered a different picture each week. Less than a year later, it seemed to me like a garden that had been there for years. The next project is the Galeries Lafayette in Berlin.

Phyto Universe Center, New York

When Patrick Alès invited me to create a vertical garden in a new space in New York that was being designed for his line of products, I immediately accepted. The garden was to be constructed at the corner of Lexington Avenue and 58th Street, a few floors up, and was to give precedence to the view one would get from the sidewalks below. And now, you can glimpse fragments of tropical forests through window panes stretching 65 feet (20 m) along the two streets. At night, the effect is particularly stunning.

58th Street
Hibiscus
Podocarpus
Hoya curtisii
Zamioculcas
Peperomia
Lexington

PHYTO UNIVERSE
&COMPANY

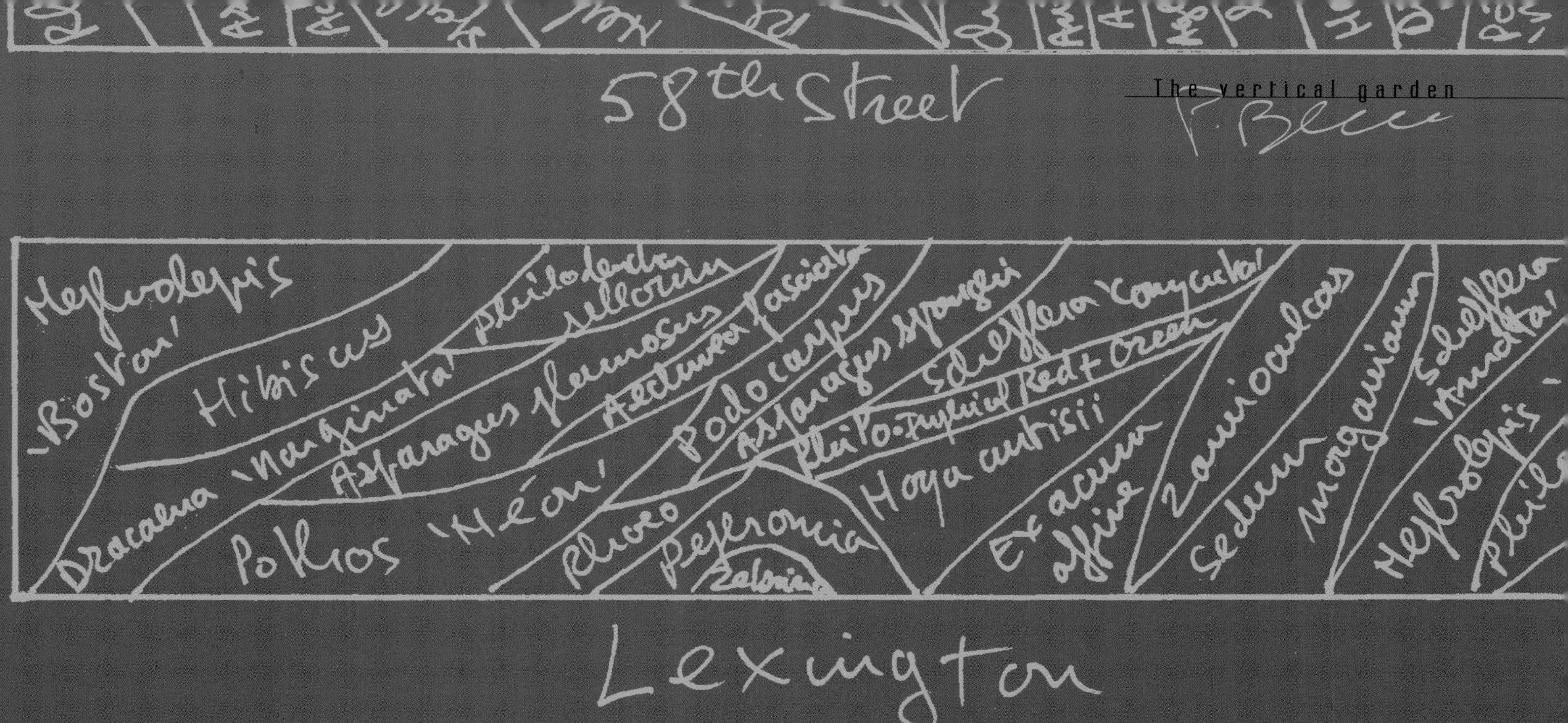

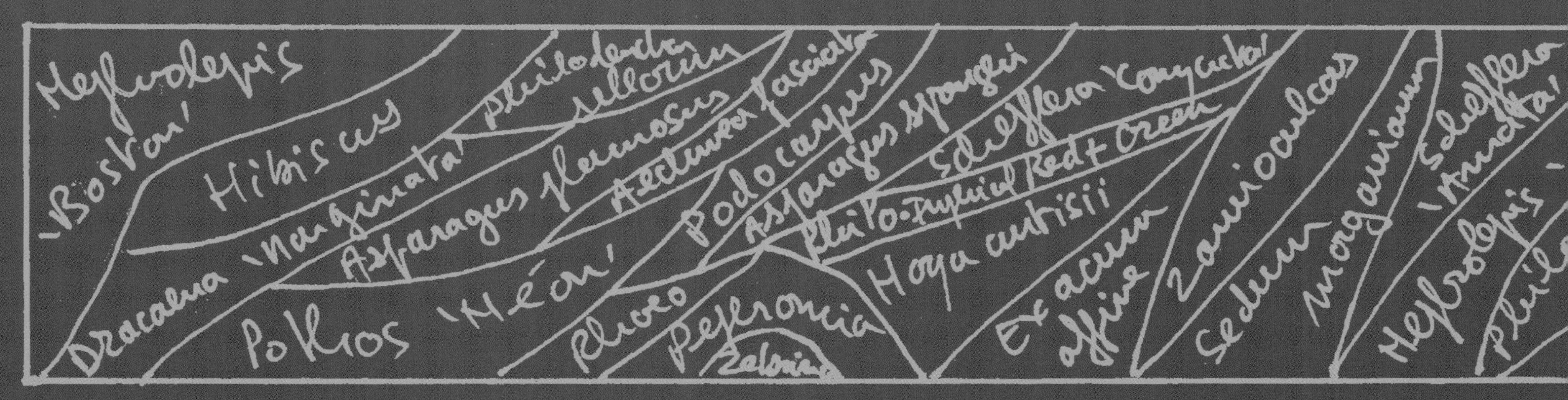

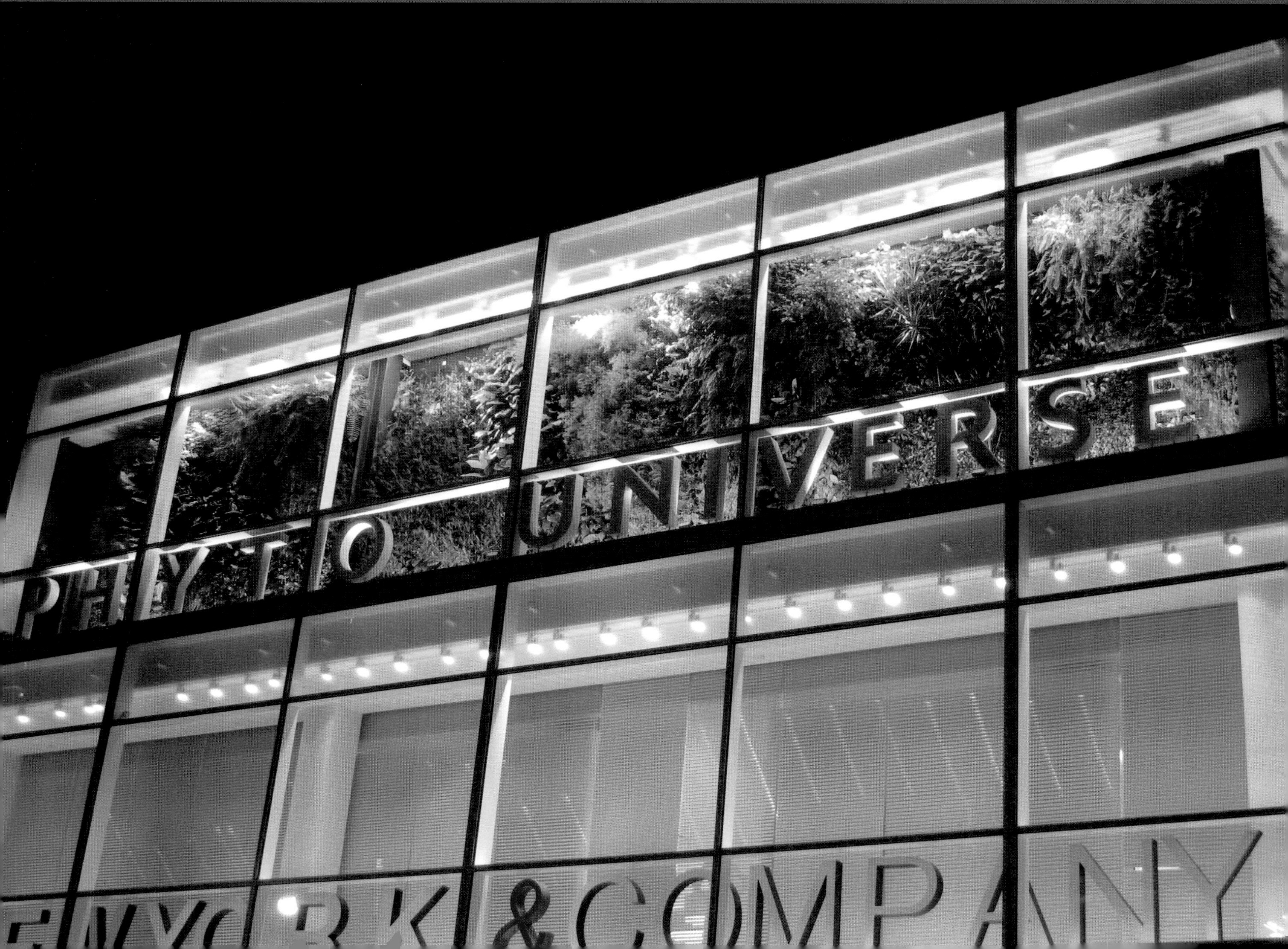

Qantas Lounges,
Sydney and Melbourne

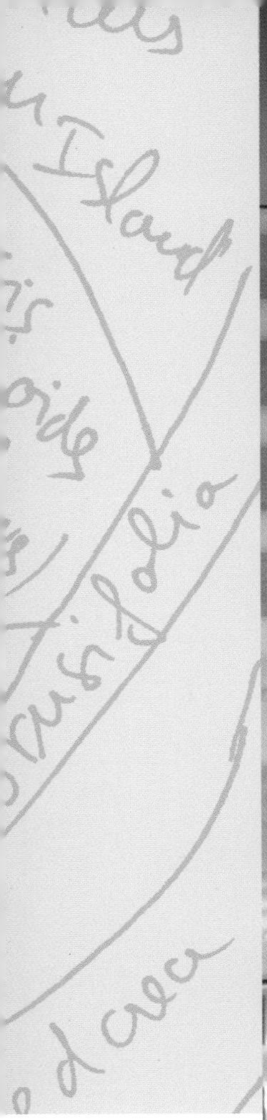

I had never been to Australia. When designer Marc Newson brought up the possibility of a very long vertical garden for the Qantas first-class lounge in Sydney, I accepted on the spot: at last, I would become acquainted with this legendary flora! And as a bonus, the project itself turned out to be fascinating because it was my largest creation to date in an enclosed space. For 165 feet (50 m), happy passengers would be able to stroll by sections of tropical forest. After a few discussions with the architect Sébastien Seguers and our Australian colleagues in charge of construction and planting, everything seemed as though it would work out quite smoothly. Indoor tropical plants are mostly cultivated in the north, in Queensland, so we needed to have them brought over to Sydney. For certain genera, such as *Medinilla,* I had the chance to work with species that I had not previously used in my gardens. There is an extensive range of plants cultivated in Australia, especially where local flora is concerned. It is obvious that Australians try to integrate this botanical richness into their cities. Certain species spontaneously grow up the walls of urban dwellings, and this was the first time in my life that I had seen such a beautiful collection of *Psilotum nudum* – on an old wall facing the Sydney opera! Later, other vertical gardens were added to the Qantas lounges in Melbourne. And several projects are currently in the works for using local plants to cover various buildings in some of the larger cities.

Concert Hall, Taipei

During my exhibition Folies végétales at the Espace EDF Electra in Paris, I became acquainted with Mr. Poimboeuf, the director of the French Institute in Taiwan, who proposed creating a vertical garden in Taipei. He knew that Mrs. Chen – a great pianist, former minister of culture, director of the Taipei Theater and Concert Hall, and admirer of French culture – would probably be interested in my work. From there everything moved quite quickly and in June 2007 I went over to survey the site. I was very warmly welcomed, and I was able to discover the astonishing richness and luxuriance of Taiwan's extremely humid, dense forests. Mrs. Chen brought me into the Concert Hall, which was being readied for its twentieth-anniversary gala in October, and said, "Here you are. Pick the spot that calls to you and create a botanical sculpture!" After visiting every corner of that immense and rather traditional building, I proposed pieces for two tall, empty walls along the main entryway. Mrs. Chen accepted my proposal and immediately introduced me to the project team so that I could explain my approach. The challenges were great, since we would have to install everything – including the plants, of course – within a space of three months. Thanks to the remarkable efficiency of everyone involved, planting began in early September, and for the inauguration in late October, the plants had already begun sprouting new leaves. We decided to entitle this particular piece "Green Symphony."

Light emitted from projectors at the top of the garden, 30 feet (10 m) high, shows off the purple areas lining the primary nerves on the *Begonia masoniana* leaves.

Primary Works

Institutions, Cities, and Collectives

Parc Floral, Paris (1994)
Jardin d'Acclimatation, Paris (1996)
Place d'Andillac (1997)
Citadelle de Doullens (1997)
Félix-Jacquier Square, Lyons (1999)
Île Saint-Germain, Issy-les-Moulineaux (1999)
Urban Park, Coulommiers (2002)
Chamber of Commerce and Industry, Lille (2003)
French Embassy, New Delhi, India (2003)
Cheminée EPAD, La Défense, Paris (2004)
Ministry of Culture, Bons-Enfants, Paris (2004)
CFDT Federation, Paris (2005)
Vinet Square, Bordeaux (2005)
Hôtel du Département, Nanterre (2005)
Market and Parking Garage, Avignon (2005)
Parliament, Brussels, Belgium (2006)
ICF Building, Bordeaux (2007)
Plaza de España, Santa Cruz de Tenerife, Spain (2008)
Apartment Façades, Rue d'Alsace, Paris (2008)
Pont-Route Max Juvenal, Aix en Provence (2008)
Bâtiment Alma, Gennevilliers (2008)
R. Boivin School, Pierrefitte (2008)
Leamouth Peninsula Building, London, England (2008)
Torre de Cristal, Madrid, Spain (Projected 2008)
Place de l'Ecole, Rue Tiquetonne, Paris (Projected 2008)
Via Verde, Rio de Janeiro, Brazil (Projected 2009)
Green Office, Meudon (Projected 2009)
Office Tower, Doha, Qatar (Projected 2009)
Landmark Tower, Abu Dhabi (Projected 2010)
Apartment Tower, Santa Monica, Los Angeles, United States (Projected)

Museums and Other Educational Sites

Cité des Sciences et de l'Industrie de la Villette, Paris (1986)
Greenhouse, Botanical Gardens, Toulouse (1996)
École du Paysage, Grasse (1996)
Le Végétarium, La Gacilly (1998)
Nave Italia Aquarium, Genoa, Italy (1998)
Maison de l'Environnement, Thiers (1998)
Vivendi Experimental Garden, Méry-sur-Oise (2000)
Palais de la Découverte, Paris (2001)
Nausicaa, Lagoon Cliff, Boulogne-sur-Mer (2003)
Nausicaa, Submerged Forest, Boulogne-sur-Mer (2004)
Quai Branly Museum, Paris (2004)
21st Century Museum of Contemporary Art, Kanazawa, Japan (2004)
Astralia, Cité de l'Espace, Toulouse (2005)
Nicolas Hulot Foundation, Boulogne-Billancourt (2006)
Caixa Forum Museum, Madrid, Spain (2007)
Private Center for Contemporary Art, Istanbul, Turkey (2007)
Concert Hall, Taipei, Taiwan (2007)
Museum of Natural History, Toulouse (2008)
Museum der Kulturen, Basel, Suisse (Projected 2009)
Miami Art Museum, Miami, Florida (Projected 2010)
Mito Art Museum, Tokyo, Japan (Projected)
XiXi Wetland Museum, Hang Zhou , China (Projected)

Exhibitions and Events

International Festival of Gardens, Chaumont-sur-Loire (1994)
In situ, in visu Exhibition, Albi (1997)
Être nature Exhibition, Cartier Foundation for Contemporary Art, Paris (1998)
Jardins des Paradis, Cordes (1999)
Senate Orangery, Paris (1999)
Le temps déborde Exhibition, Le Blanc-Mesnil (1999)
Les Mondes lumière Exhibition, Espace EDF Electra, Paris (2002)
"La Robe végétale," Fashion Show with Jean-Paul Gaultier, Paris (2002)
Van Cleef and Arpels, SIHH Exhibition, Geneva, Switzerland (2002)
Garden Cavern, La Roche-Guyon (2002)
Green Living Room, Paris (2002)
L'Orgart, for the La Source de Gérard Garouste Foundation (2002)
"Maison & Objets" Salon, Paris (2003)
Festival des Deux Rives, Strasbourg (2004)
Chapada do Araripe Exhibition, São Paulo, Brazil (2004)
Sale temps sur la planète Exhibition, Boulogne-sur-Mer (2005)
Commissioner for the *Folies végétales* Exhibition, Espace EDF Electra, Paris (2007)
Airs de Paris Exhibition, Centre Georges Pompidou, Paris (2007)
Afterglow Exhibition, Lacoste (2007)
Stella McCartney Fashion Show, Paris (2007)

Commercial Establishments

Yves Rocher Boutiques, La Défense, Paris; Belle Épine; Créteil (1998–2002)
HypoVereinsbank, Munich, Germany (1999)
Bon Génie Boutique, Geneva, Switzerland (2001)
Les Passages Shopping Center, Boulogne-Billancourt (2001)
Marithé and François Girbaud Boutique, Paris (2002)
DDB Headquarters, Paris (2002)
Babyliss Headquarters, Montrouge (2002)
Marithé and François Girbaud Boutique, New York, New York (2003)
Law Offices, Luxembourg City, Luxembourg (2003)
Samsung Headquarters, Seoul, South Korea (2003)
Marithé and François Girbaud Boutique, Osaka, Japan (2004)
iGuzzini Illuminazione Showroom, Paris (2004)
Ternes Parking Garage, Paris (2005)
Ken Club Spa, Paris (2005)
Andaska Quick Silver Boutique, Biarritz (2005)
Siam Paragon Shopping Center, Bangkok, Thailand (2005)
Emporium Shopping Center, Bangkok, Thailand (2005)
Espace Weleda, Paris (2006)
Les Quatre Temps Shopping Center, La Défense, Paris (2006)
Andaska Boutique, Briançon (2006)
Phyto Universe, New York, New York (2006)
Club Med, Paris (2007)
BHV Homme, Paris (2007)
Esplanade Shopping Center, Bangkok, Thailand (2007)
Omotesando Gyre, Tokyo, Japan (2007)
Club Med, Brussels, Belgium (2007)
Business Center, Tbilisi, Georgia (2007)
Sales-Lentz Travel Agency, Luxembourg (2007)
Les Quatre Temps Shopping Center, Annex, La Défense, Paris (2008)
Frankfurt International Salon, Press Center, Germany (2008)
Rolex Showroom, Milan, Italy (2008)
Trussardi, Piazza della Scala, Milan, Italy (2008)
Galeries Lafayette, Berlin, Germany (2008)
Pacha Club, Kings Cross and Victoria, London, England (Projected 2008)
Boutique, Charlotte, North Carolina (Projected 2008)
360 Shopping Center, Kuwait City, Kuwait (Projected 2008)

Hotels, Restaurants, Lounges

Hôtel Pershing Hall, Paris (2001)
Hôtel Il Palazetto, Cannes (2001)
La Bastide Restaurant, Los Angeles, California (2002)
Hotel Byblos, Saint-Tropez (2002)
Delannoy Offices, Paris (2006)
Qantas Lounge, Melbourne, Australia (2007)
Qantas Lounge, Sydney, Australia (2007)
St. Moritz Brasserie Bar, Barcelona, Spain (2008)
Al'Patatrie Restaurant, Amiens (2008)
Lan Restaurant, Shanghai, China (2008)
Cavalieri Hotel, Pinerolo (2008)
Ornithorynque, Hotel Paris (Projected 2008)
Forum des Arènes, Nîmes (Projected 2008)
Dream Hotel, New York, New York (Projected 2008)
Grand Mercure Hotel, Bangkok, Thailand (Projected 2008)
Novotel, Saint-Quentin-en-Yvelines (Projected 2009)
Praterstrasse Shopping Center and Hotel, Vienna, Austria (Projected 2009)
Hotel and Apartments, Ibiza, Spain (Projected 2009)

Private Installations

Numerous installations both indoors (apartments, basements, pools...) and outdoors (terraces, walls, and various rehabilitated façades), in France and throughout the world.

"Le Mur végétal" (the vertical garden) is copyright-protected.
Web site : www.verticalgardenpatrickblanc.com

Drawings by Patrick Blanc

Photos by Patrick Blanc except: © Véronique Lalot: pp. 3, 4, 84, 92 (bottom left), 93 (top), 95, 105 (middle), 110, 111 (top), 114, 115 (bottom), 122, 123 (left), 125 (middle and bottom), 127 (bottom), 128-129, 130-131, 134 (bottom left and right), 135 (top left), 146, 147 (top), 148-149, 152-153, 154-155, 156-157, 164-165, 180-181, 182, 184, 185 (bottom); © Pascal Héni: pp. 2, 6, 10, 88, 92 (top right), 94 (bottom), 99 (middle left), 104, 105 (left), 118-119, 140 (top left), 177 (top); © Janewit Lakhumlek: pp. 85, 88, 90; © Charkkrayut Phijarana: p. 105 (right); © Éric Ossart: p. 106 (bottom); © D.R.: pp. 151, 158, 188, 189

Originally published in French under the title
LE MUR VÉGÉTAL: De la Nature à la Ville

Printed in Korea

For information about permission to reproduce selections from this book, write to Permissions, W. W. Norton & Company, Inc.
500 Fifth Avenue, New York, NY 10110

For information about special discounts for bulk purchases, please contact W. W. Norton Special Sales at specialsales@wwnorton.com or 800-233-4830

Composition by Joe Lops
Production manager: Leeann Graham

Library of Congress Cataloging-in-Publication Data

Blanc, Patrick.
[Mur végétal. English]
The vertical garden : from nature to the city / Patrick Blanc ; preface by Jean Nouvel ; photography by the author and Véronique Lalot ; translation by Gregory P. Bruhn.
p. cm.
"Originally published in French under the title Le Mur végétal : de la nature à la ville."
ISBN 978-0-393-73259-7 (hardcover)
1. Vertical gardening. 2. Climbing plants. I. Lalot, Véronique. II. Title.
SB463.5.B53 2008
684.1'8—dc22
2008010996

ISBN 13: 978-0-393-73259-7

W. W. Norton & Company, Inc., 500 Fifth Avenue
New York, N.Y. 10110
www.wwnorton.com

W. W. Norton & Company Ltd., Castle House
75/76 Wells Street, London W1T 3QT

0 9 8 7 6 5 4 3 2